The Truth:

The Truth:

Turning the Lights Back On In America

A nation of lost sheep . . .

**Want to change what they teach
in your history class?**

Here's how!

JOHN H. ZAUGG

 authorHOUSE®

AuthorHouse™ LLC
1663 Liberty Drive
Bloomington, IN 47403
www.authorhouse.com
Phone: 1-800-839-8640

Published by AuthorHouse   02/17/2014

ISBN: 978-1-4918-3771-9 (sc)
ISBN: 978-1-4918-3773-3 (e)

Library of Congress Control Number: 2013920957

Table of Contents

What will be required to get the thousand-pound gorilla off our backs?

Public policies that rely on force and intimidation, allegedly to solve problems, and are used against everyone, including our children and people around the globe, will result in a very dangerous world.

"Each must for himself alone decide what is right and what is wrong, and which course is patriotic and which isn't. You cannot shirk this and be a man. To decide against your convictions is to be an unqualified and inexcusable traitor, both to yourself and to your country. If you alone of all the nation shall decide one way, and that way be the right way according to your convictions, you have done your duty by yourself and by your country—hold up your head! You have nothing to be ashamed of."

Mark Twain, 1835-1910

A nation running on empty

Money doesn't grow on trees.

*We have got to stand for something
or we will fall for anything.*

Preface

This book is written for those who want to know what will be required to turn the lights back on in America.

It's not complicated. Being human means our lives and choices are guided by our values and principles. We either live like responsible adults or descend down a slippery slope—that is the choice we are making. Individual liberty without moral values does not solve America's problem. We must answer an essential question: what values must we learn and revere if we are to restore the future for our children?

Manifest in the Declaration of Independence is a very simple message: *People should not, and need not, live like obedient subjects.* Today, if you look at what is happening in the United States and how we conduct our public policies, you'll see that the message from the American people is: *We intend to live like subjects, obedient and subservient to a welfare/warfare state.*

Insanity: doing the same thing over and over
again and expecting different results.
Albert Einstein

Just like a drug addict, America has become a culture addicted to massive government. We are headed down this path of perpetual servitude because we have never had a discussion about what is required to live like "people" instead of "subjects." What does being human mean? What is the nature of man and the foundation of civilization that makes personal liberty so important? America was not supposed to be a nation reliant on politicians. First, let's be honest: the politicians are not doing a very good job. And second, it's our responsibility to define what kind of nation and people we should be.

What we see happening in the United States is nothing new. This is not the first time a civilization has faced collapse.

> They take our very flesh, and they hate and despise us. And who shall say we are worthy of more? When a government becomes powerful it is destructive, extravagant, and violent; it is a usurer which takes bread from innocent mouths and deprives honorable men of their substance, for votes with which to perpetuate itself.
> Marcus Tullius Cicero (106-43 BC), Roman statesman, philosopher, and orator

We are headed for collapse for much the same reason that the Roman Empire collapsed. The problem then and now, no one wants to talk about the real problems or their solutions. The question I am posing is this: Are you prepared to discuss what kind of nation and people we should be?

In my lifetime I have never experienced a book or professor honestly assessed the challenges and flaws that now face us. Turn off the television. Put down the cell phone. Here is the discussion we need to have if we are to restore the American dream.

The question is do we want to live and be treated like people? To live like people we must refuse to support, condone, or cooperate with intimidation or harm inflicted on anyone without legitimate justification. When faced with criminal behavior and crimes against humanity, we must refuse to remain silent, refuse to cooperate, refuse to be complicit in the inhumanity. Living like people is what the concept of a free society was intended to represent. Whether it is terrorism, crime, or corruption of any kind, we have to talk about what is undermining our country's prospects for enduring peace and prosperity. It will require some degree of courage, but we really have no other choice. We must define and uphold the values, convictions, and principles upon which our success as humans depends. Those *moral values* are what will make the difference between success and failure, on both an individual and a national level.

Young people, this book is about your future. You're getting an education and learning how to become competent adults, but the knowledge you need to make the most of your opportunities in life is being deliberately distorted. You need to understand that teachers, professors, politicians, and news media deliberately remain silent on the most crucial challenges facing us. They do not want you to question the meaningless debates, reporting, and education to which you are being subjected. You're being lied to because they want to control your choices, and your money. In other words, it is your life they want to control. What they secretly (or not-so-secretly) intend to preserve is the welfare/warfare system. The "left" wants to preserve the benevolent government ideology; the "right" wants to preserve the military-corporate complex. The nation (modern America) is being misled by a bunch of emperors up on stage wearing fancy clothes made of invisible thread. America was supposed to represent everyone's opportunity in life. Instead, you're living in a society in which you will be used, abused, enslaved, and militarized, bearing the burdens that my generation has so relentlessly and unapologetically imposed. It has got to stop, and only by standing up to the corruption will we turn the lights back on in America.

Young people what follows is a discussion of America's underlying problems and their solutions. Here is why you're growing up with a thousand-pound gorilla on your backs, and why today's politicians can accomplish little more than "kicking the can down the road."

My generation has taken America down a path of growing complacency and servitude, and it's not working. As result, just like the Roman Empire, we are headed for a historic collapse.

When you finish reading this book you're going to be smarter than your average college professor, because you will be able to talk about and answer the questions: *What kind of people are we?* and, *How do we become the best we can be?*

To become the best we can be we have to learn a very simple lesson.

We cannot solve our country's problems by relying on government, legislation, and politicians. Ultimately, such subservience and obedience only makes matters worse. To become our best, as individuals and as a nation, we have to restore the confidence, trust, and expectations that we each must make of our lives as members of the greatest nation on earth.

1   A Nation of Lost Sheep

> The mass of mankind has not been born with
> saddles on their backs, nor a favored few booted
> and spurred, ready to ride them legitimately, by the
> grace of God.
> Thomas Jefferson, third US president

All of us should live like *people*—not like doormats being pushed around by those with boots and spurs. Finger pointing and blame laying are not honest solutions. Waiting on or counting on government to solve societal problems is the flaw destroying your future. Do you know why humanity has repeatedly descended into wars, dictatorships, and poverty? Because people didn't realize what disasters they were being led into. But ignorance is no excuse.

> America will never be destroyed from the
> outside. If we falter and lose our freedoms, it will be
> because we destroyed ourselves.
> Abraham Lincoln, sixteenth US president

We should live in a free society for one very simple reason: human nature requires us to take responsibility for everything we say and do. We must not rely on force and lies in dealing with one another. If we want to live like responsible adults, we have to learn, validate, teach, and revere those personal expectations and shared principles that make human success unstoppable. Absent those convictions, society ultimately degenerates into some form of civil and financial collapse.

I like to think that during the decline of the Roman Empire, there were citizens who saw what was destroying their lives and knew how to make the changes necessary to preserve the civil society. The problem was, no one listened, or they were brutally assaulted by government agents to use brute force, to keep protesters, whistle-blowers, and other aggrieved citizens silent. For decades after the fall of the Roman Empire, people longed for its return, because that civilization had provided something that healthy, life-loving people wanted and cherished. Today I see essentially the same thing happening.

I have concluded that *solving problems* is what makes us human, and that *faking it* makes us incompetent and less than human. What we endure today is endless talk about our problems with no meaningful substance. In order to solve a problem, one has to identify its underlying cause. So let's start the problem-solving process. Here is some evidence of why we Americans are rendered so gullible. It serves as an example of the mentality (flawed moral presumptions) we live with today, which is the opposite of what being fully human requires.

> . . . . producers and non-producers are required to help the "Others." Government is the enabling instrument to bring out the caring tendency of people who do not know each other. To attain minimum standards of decency as a right for people

rather than as a voluntary gift to them. In other words, the government serves as a redistributive mechanism that stops the society from flying apart for economic reasons.

Marcus G. Raskin, *The Common Good: Its Politics, Policies and Philosophy,* 1986

What do you think about the above quote? Do you agree? How you care for the "Others" may be the most important decision you make in your life! Should caring for "others" be voluntary or an obligation imposed by force and legislation?

There is no emperor or bureaucratic system that relieves us of the responsibility of exercising personal judgment. What the above quote promotes is mandated sharing *to attain minimum standards of decency.* The thousand-pound gorilla you live with today is the result. We are deliberately being led down a path that is resulting in the erosion of the American Dream.

We are taught today that people cannot manage their own lives or make healthy choices or even define a set of moral values; because we are such dolts. Thus, we must live reliant on and subservient to some authority to attain minimum standards of decency. That is the redistributive mechanism, mental cloud we now live in. Consider this quote from Professor Michael Sandel, whose course on "Justice" is one of the most popular and influential at Harvard University.

I do not think that freedom of choice—even freedom of choice under fair conditions—is an adequate basis for a just society.

Michael J. Sandel, PhD, *Justice: What Is the Right Thing to Do?* 2009

The real problem is not just that professors hold such contempt for personal liberty, but that most of them do not even believe there is a definable set of principles that should guide our lives. They actually believe that people cannot solve society's problems. In their judgment, only benevolent government can guide and sustain civilization. Here is more evidence of how Professor Sandel views people.

> The mere fact that a group of people in the past agreed to a constitution is not enough to make the constitution just.

> No actual social or constitution convention, however representative, is guaranteed to produce fair terms of social cooperation.

Today's intellectuals are convinced that you and I are incapable of defining principles, a constitution, or shared values. But we know that as humans, we are all capable of making moral choices, and we must build our lives by exercising our human potential. I'm convinced we (people) can agree upon a *just constitution* and can learn to live together as competent citizens. The Founding Fathers had it right. The question is: Why have we gone so far astray from the ideals—the inherent confidence in human nature—upon which they intended to built the nation?

Defining the underlying problem in American society is where the discussion must start. Here is evidence of the underlying problem, from Sidney Hook an Emeritus Professor at New York University and Senior Research Fellow at the Hoover Institution.

Scientists do not disagree about the validity
of specific laws that have been established, nor
do mathematicians disagree about the validity of
specific theorems. But there is not a single piece of
philosophical knowledge, not a single philosophical
proposition on which philosophers are all agreed.

If progress is measured in the same way as it
is in fields like medicine or physics, by increase in
systematized knowledge and control, then we must
acknowledge that there has been no progress.

It envelopes even those who, on skeptical
or meta-ethical grounds, have concluded that
philosophy has nothing cognitively meaningful to
say about human values.

Sidney Hook, PhD, *Philosophy and Public
Policy,* 1980

Can you fathom this? You now live in a society where
highly respected commentators and professors teach
that . . .

- □ government must redistribute society's wealth,
- □ freedom is unworkable and unjust, and
- □ modern philosophy has nothing meaningful to say
  about human values.

What nonsense! If philosophy has nothing to offer
when it comes to human values, what does that leave for us
to choose from for moral guidance? And yet we are entirely
capable of making healthy choices and solving problems;
mankind has survived for thousands of years by doing so.

Apparently our college professors have no idea how people succeeded for generations, but we sit in lecture halls, listening to these idiots.

How are we to understand, let alone resolve problems like drug abuse, growing poverty, or endless wars if our leaders can't even agree on . . .

- ☐ what values to recommend,
- ☐ what is the proper role of government, or
- ☐ what economic system makes prosperity possible?

How would you answer those questions? Do you think a community can prosper without agreeing on basic moral values? Isn't that what America was supposed to represent—a set of values? Maybe the blindness and societal problems we're enduring is the choice we have made, and now we have to re-examine the fallacies and flawed ideologies, the flawed foundation of modern society.

That is why I want to live in a free society where people recognize the need to talk to one another. Instead we are so demeaned and mistreated and presumed so incompetent that we must live like subjects of the anointed rulers in some kind of fantasyland. And anyone who dares to speak the truth may end up imprisoned or hiding in some foreign country to avoid US prosecution.

Here is more evidence of the underlying problem from Thomas Nagel, professor of philosophy at New York University and author of several works in moral and political philosophy.

> The things for which people are morally judged are determined in more ways than we first realize by what is beyond their control. And,

> when the seemingly natural requirement of fault
> or responsibility is applied in light of these facts,
> it leaves few pre-reflective judgments intact.
> Ultimately, nothing or almost nothing about what a
> person does seems to be under his control.
> Thomas Nagel, PhD, *Moral Questions*, 1991

What this professor is saying is that people (i.e., you and I) are not capable of making moral judgments. His contention that "almost nothing about what a person does seems to be under his control" defines the blindness we are now faced with. This means we are, by nature, idiots, incapable of doing the right thing. Modern philosophy has no vision or principles or values, or confidence in people. That is the underlying problem with our society. How can we claim to be competent adults if we cannot define solutions to the growing inhumanity we see around us? Today we are taught that we are incapable of exercising personal integrity, just and competent behavior because there are no qualities of character we should revere, teach, and practice in our lives. Thus, we must live relying on rule makers, emperors, and bureaucrats to make our judgments for us. This lack of trust in ourselves, our presumed inherent incompetence, means we must live like subjects of some master authority—and the growing inhumanities and reliance on force and violence persist.

What does modern philosophy teach us? That we cannot be certain about anything.

> What must a brain do in order to believe a
> certain statement is true or false? We currently have
> no idea. We cannot live by reason alone.
> Sam Harris, *The End of Faith: Religion, Terror,
> and the Future of Reason*, 2004

We do not know, nor have we ever known, whether we are right or wrong. Life's great uncertainty principle is that no one can ever be sure whether he is ultimately correct or incorrect in his views of the nature and purpose of life in the universe.

Kalman H. Silvert, *The Reason for Democracy,* 1977

The issue that underlies our politics and our society in the 1990s is the moral, social and cultural erosion of the past quarter century in American life. It is the gradual disappearance of safe streets, stable families, secure employment, and the enduring relationships with relatives, neighbors, merchants and co-workers that make an orderly life possible. It is the unraveling of the strands of community—of what we are now calling civil society. There is no easy way to reverse it. Government cannot order moral revival. But some policies are worse than others. Entrusting our future to an uncontrolled and amoral free market may be the worst of all. Nor does it make much sense to pronounce the word "choice" over and over like a mantra. Communities aren't built on individual choice.

Alan Ehrenhalt, *The New York Times,* Nov. 19, 1995

Your subconscious mind controls all the vital processes of your body and knows the answer to all problems. Your subconscious mind is one with infinite intelligence and boundless wisdom. Your

thoughts of health, vitality, and perfection operate
through the one universal subjective mind.

Joseph Murphy, PhD, *The Power of Your
Subconscious Mind*, 2000

These are examples of the pervasive disrespect for
people among the American intellectual elite. As result we
are a nation running on empty. Let's be clear: if an amoral,
laissez-faire economy means living without any personal
values, chaos will indeed be the result. The lesson we must
learn is that no government or free market, no amount of
freedom, no amount of subjective rationalizations, *relieves
any of us of the need for moral values.* In fact, freedom
recognizes the need for values, principles, and ideals as the
foundation of our success. Freedom and the free market are
not means of escape from personal responsibility. Freedom
is the recognition that only by taking responsibility can
each of us function as a competent adult.

Without values, life becomes nothing more than a
game, a means of deceiving ourselves into believing that
we are doing the right thing while ignoring the growing
suffering and disparity all around us. It means being led
down a path without understanding where that path leads. It
means looking good and going shopping, but never having
a discussion about what the concept of "right" and "wrong"
means.

Abraham Lincoln was exactly right.

If we falter and lose our freedoms, it will be
because we destroyed ourselves.

There is an alternative to self-destruction—and it is not
complicated. I am confident that we are entirely capable

of turning the lights back on in America and restoring our children's future.

> The essential threat, the true and genuine threat at the heart of all the others, is the threat to the individual. This fact often remains unseen and unremarked. We are, after all, or we once were, said to be a nation of individuals, to value individualism, to pride ourselves on our individuality, and we live, of course, in a nation whose founding was dedicated to the protection of individual freedoms. But so much of that has now been eroded, so much of it has been made a sham, so much has been bent, twisted, numbed, used, channeled, undervalued, pandered to, fawned over, flattered, demeaned, made un-self-conscious, programmatically under-nourished, and again and again and again, so endlessly and unremittingly exploited as an easy means to ever baser and baser and baser ends—that the damage, if nothing else, has grown to the point of having become threatening to the nation's very life.
>
> Erick Larsen, *A Nation Gone Blind: America in an Age of Simplification and Deceit*, 2006

How does it feel to be presumed so incompetent that we must live dependent on a welfare state? How does it feel to be told the only way Americans can have affordable health care or get an education is if they are provided by government? How does it feel to live in a country that believes the way to protect and preserve civilization or world peace is with a hundred military bases around the globe and a thousand nuclear bombs ready to be launched at a moment's notice? How does it feel to be living as obedient servants of the military-industrial, corporate, welfare complex? My generation has basically taken the concepts of personal liberty, individual responsibility, and the US Constitution and flushed them down the toilet.

Here is a columnist who describes Americans' current inability to meaningfully discuss or reach agreement on anything.

> Secularists who insist that the questions of morality be answered on the basis of "reason" are merely using a different word to describe what self-consciously religious people call "the moral law" or "God's will," or something similar. And since secularists are no more able to agree upon what "reason" requires in regard to controversial moral issues than religious people are able to agree on the substance of the moral law or God's will, invoking reason when arguing about subjects such as abortion is exactly as useful as invoking the authority of sacred scripture or of the pope—which is to say, such invocations will be quite effective in convincing those who already agree with the speaker, but will otherwise fall upon deaf ears.
>
> Paul Campos, *Rocky Mountain News,* January 22, 2002

Paul Campos is right. What are the prospects of a community working together to solve problems if people cannot communicate or agree on anything? What kind of world will we endure if we cannot talk to one another? And by "talk" I don't mean lay blame or point fingers, or kicking the can down the road. Talking to one another means to articulate the *vision* and *principles* upon which our children's future absolutely depends.

Are we ready to stand up? Are we prepared to act like adults, or are we going to continue to get by the way con artists do, faking it to hide our moral emptiness?

In writing this book, I am motivated by a passion to help forge a new direction for America. I understand that forging a new path and validating shared principles (or reviving old and forgotten principles) is not something people want to talk about. I understand that the views I express here are not going to be popular, especially among older generations. I respect those who disagree with me, and I hope they will consider what I have to offer with an open mind. We are standing on the deck of a sinking ship, and it is my generation that has brought us to this sorry state of affairs. If the problems we now face as a society were understood by the vast majority of Americans, we would be resolving the unnecessary human suffering that now confronts us. In other words, *if* we practiced and agreed upon an accepted set of valid principles, we would not be confronted with such doubt about our future. Human success is not the manifestation of some mythical ideology or some biased, convoluted political agenda. What is different about my approach is that I base my solutions on the recognition that character is just as real, definable, and important as any other challenge faced by mankind. Humans are capable of living like problem solvers. America was founded on the best of human nature. I put my trust in people to make intelligent choices. But what I've came to realize is that in order to defend our personal liberty or behave like problem solvers, we must understand what being good, just, fair—what being human—means and requires. And once we learn how to live like problem solvers, those emperors, who insist on running (ruining) our lives, are going to get laughed off the stage.

So let's grow up, stop laying blame, and do what has to be done. Here is the question we might want to start with.

The Source of Moral Knowledge

What values should guide how we make choices? Do such values even exist? If so, where do they come from?

As we enter the twenty-first century there is no agreement among Americans about what's "right" or "wrong." We need to understand that there is no crystal ball or political system that can absolve us from defining a shared moral compass. There is no agreement, in fact, there seems to be a mindset that we cannot or *should not* teach moral values in our schools. What if society's moral blindness is the yellow brick road leading to disaster? So let's do what healthy adults must do and define the moral values that sustains humanity. There are a number of possible answers. Either our moral values are handed down and imposed by some master authority; or they are discovered, tested, proven, articulated, and validated by mankind through the reasoning process. You may disagree with this analysis, but you deserve to consider, at least, the possibility that adhering to personal convictions is *entirely within the realm of our capability and responsibility.* There is no master authority or benevolent government that relieves citizens of moral responsibility.

All knowledge is acquired through the validating, reasoning process. For those adults who are turned off by such an act of personal accountability, I have some questions: Are you willing to talk about how our beliefs and values are tested and proven? Can we agree on what is meant by "problem solving"? If people are not capable of defining the principles they trust in, then how can they be held responsible or accountable for their actions? What does being "human" mean? What is the truth, and how do we recognize it? Can we live like responsible adults and not answer those kinds of questions?

Is relying on some authority to establish our value system our only option? Is morality something generated outside our own nature and judgment? If you choose to live dependent and obedient, that is your choice. Do you decide how you will live, or do you just obey (when you feel you have to) the rules and rule makers?

Here's the underlying question: What does personal responsibility mean?

I base my views on the conviction that people, each of us, is capable of being the best we could be. Therefore, the *pursuit of happiness* requires each of us to define the moral guidelines that enable us to realize our highest aspirations. Values matter. Is there anything more important to us than what we each achieve in our lifetime? Is building a better future something we should care about? Could it be that the persistent problems we face, as a society, are entirely of our own making, the result of flawed excuses that must be questioned and corrected to restore our confidence in ourselves? I hope you're beginning to see that, at the very least, we should take a good look at ourselves in the mirror.

We need to face the possibility that all the suffering we currently endure is a consequence of flawed moral premises and not some affliction that dooms our chances at human success. My point is this: *we can choose not to live like obedient doormats.* Thus, we must identify those flawed assumptions and articulate the moral values that make human success possible. We should have had this discussion fifty years ago, but better late than never.

And here is the problem: if we don't have this discussion and define that moral compass, then we are left guided by . . . what? What if, without convictions, we fall for anything, including living in a moral fog?

Should people be required to live in service to the greater good, as *thy brother's keeper*? Is mandatory caring for people (benevolent government) a necessary, legitimate function of government? Are people capable of solving problems guided by their own judgment, abilities, desires, and aspirations? How do you answer those questions?

The underlying tenet of this book is that civilizations are built on personal values, not mandatory (forced) obedience of any kind. This book rejects the false argument that people are flawed and must live dependent on divine intervention, social safety nets, or authoritarian governments. Civilization is built on the understanding that people, each of us, can be competent, proud, trustworthy problem solvers and positive contributors to humanity. Yes, we can talk about and agree upon a "vision" that recognizes the potential in each of us. Let's be clear: we have put a man on the moon, but we continue to endure persistent war and inhumanity here on earth. There is no justification for such suffering. Those intellectuals, commentators, and politicians don't want to admit it, but we are not a bunch of idiots, zombies, or doormats. (Actually we *are* idiots as long as we are duped into believing their lies and propaganda.)

One view of civilization rests on a basic respect for the rights and responsibilities of people to manage and provide for their own needs and welfare, I call it living like "people." The other view assumes people should rely on benevolent rule makers. I call that living like "doormats." One defines the foundation of a free society; the other is used as the justification for mandated subservience. America was supposed to represent the right of each citizen to manage his or her own life. Our intellectual leaders have compromised that ideal over the past decades, so that today it is almost impossible to find a politician, author, or commentator who can explain how human nature and qualities of character make freedom so life sustaining. The choice we face is whether to live like responsible adults, addressing and solving problems on a daily basis, or to live like couch potatoes, playing the system without regard for the unintended consequences, the harm we are responsible for.

There are authors, commentators, politicians who advocate for personal liberty, but what is absence is any discussion or agreement on what being free means—that living as adults in a free society requires a shared moral compass.

People are capable of living moral lives and making healthy choices. Contrary to what we are taught, people are not inherently helpless, evil, or flawed and therefore dependent on some authority. People are capable of exercising responsibility. People don't need forgiveness or salvation; they don't need to be submissive to a bunch of bureaucrats. What they need, desperately, is *respect* for their own potential and the *knowledge* upon which to build self-confidence. Self-doubt is what renders people irresponsible and inclined to live as subjects of phony ideologies. Personal inspiration and confidence are the guiding light of people of character. A moral compass that recognizes the individual's ability and potential to live like a competent human is the prerequisite to achieving the best within each of us. But in America today it is presumed that we cannot trust ourselves or one another and must live as subjects of the rule makers.

It is a simple but profound concept: responsible adults work together to solve their own problems and will not tolerate threats, intimidation, or laws that claim to relieve people of their problems and responsibilities. A free society does not coerce, compel, or intimidate. It does not provide, plan, or think for people. It protects people's right to take responsibility for their own lives, needs, welfare, and happiness. This revolutionary ideal has been the guiding light that has made America so successful. Personal character forms the foundation of human progress and mutual respect. Our potential as competent humans who acquire and exercise qualities of character is the light that has been extinguished.

We do not need to travel down the path to servitude. We can live like responsible adults with confidence, trust, and respect for everyone.

> A wise and frugal government, which shall restrain men from injuring one another, which shall leave them otherwise free to regulate their own pursuits of industry and improvement, and shall not take from the mouth of labor the bread it has earned.
>
> Thomas Jefferson, 1801

People do not develop good character if they are taught to live obedient to some authority. Such obedience and dependence will only make people more obstinate and disrespectful, and potentially a burden on society. Instead of living by their own good judgment, people will learn to use laws, subsidies, and handouts to their advantage, resulting in corporate corruption, black markets, a welfare state, and organized crime. We live in a society of rules and rulers because the only recognized standards of behavior are a maze of meddlesome, subjective, contradictory policies and edicts. We have become a nation where the only "solution" to a societal problem is to rely on the political process. Our reliance on laws and rule makers means we are being treated like peons, because we allow such abuse and contempt for our potential and rights. Freedom cannot be preserved with legislation. Only responsible adults can make a society work successfully.

History can serve as a lesson for everything we do as a nation. Look at every totalitarian dictatorship in history, including racist, fascist, and communist countries. They are plagues that people were led into, entirely avoidable and preventable *had people known better.* But these plagues occurred because people didn't know better, because they were never taught what values sustain human progress. They never learned the personal convictions that release human potential. Instead they believed and trusted in their rulers, who turned out to be con artists. Instead of exercising their own moral convictions, people blindly relied on emperors wearing fancy clothes. People were taught to submit and obey instead of making healthy choices and living like problem solvers.

Success is the result of individual initiative combined with voluntary cooperation. But personal liberty does not guarantee success. When humanity is not guided by moral convictions, mankind (as history documents) descends into disparity, exploitation, corruption, environmental pollution, and wars. When a community does not teach ethics, it will not preserve humanity, justice, the environment, or personal liberty. A free market simply recognizes that people *should* assume control of their own destiny. If people act like couch potatoes, eating junk food, elbowing their way up to the public trough, living in debt, behaving like parasites and bullies—they are destroying their own and their children's future.

A declining standard of living (health crises and economic desperation) will be the first indicators of America's underlying moral decay. This erosion of citizens' well-being should warn us of the growing number of character flaws being embraced by the American people and our leaders. For a brief history of how we got to where we are, turn to the appendix.

It is apparent to anyone who looks up from his or her cell phone. America's successes are proof of what's possible when people hold certain ideals, values, and principles and apply them in their lives. The recent economic success of China is a result of similar values used by an authoritarian government that allows people to learn and exercise personal initiative. But because of the inherent corruption and absence of respect for citizens rights, in Chinese society, that country has created a financial bubble that will collapse and be followed by civil unrest. People are capable of controlling and managing their own lives responsibly. We must understand that people are not inherently moronic; they don't require some authority to think or provide for them. People can exercise moral responsibility when given the opportunity and some basic guidance on what constitutes responsible behavior. It's time to take the blinders off, both in America and around the globe.

This is where intellectual leaders are supposed to stand up. Instead, they insist on telling us there are no clear standards of right and wrong, no verifiable principles that should guide us, no universal truths or certainty about anything involving human behavior.

When public discourse looks more like a family feud instead of a process of honest communication, when we cannot solve basic problems, it is time to ask ourselves why. Why is communication a process of spin: framing the argument, offering subjective definitions, and proselytizing? When human discourse resembles advertising more than education, how can people develop self-confidence? Advertising persuades by narrowing and distorting a subject, focusing on sound bites, seducing people into becoming mindless consumers. Education, in contrast, explains and clarifies information and facilitates human abilities. Education should teach us how to distinguish truth from propaganda, self-worth from self-abdication; advertising misleads us with creative schemes to get us to buy into whatever is being sold. A coherent argument identifies concepts crucial to problem solving, to understanding the potential benefits of a recommended course of action; instead we are taught that there is no such thing as personal responsibility, no set of shared ideals we can all agree upon. If our teachers and professors promoted the idea of personal accountability as the foundation of modern living, we would be living in a totally different kind of world. We may not know or care what is being taught in our philosophy departments, but if we passively accept living in a world of contrived beliefs, we are just as guilty of intellectual fraud as those professors.

Instead of living in this moral gray area, either remaining silent or descending into a yelling match, let's start the discussion that could change everyone's lives. Parents and adults who are reading this book, you will learn things about your children you never imagined.

You'll find out that our youth are well aware of the problems facing America, and you'll see what kind of pain, loneliness, anger, and emptiness they are enduring. You will discover the importance of personal convictions to developing lasting relationships. Friends and loved ones are far more important than wealth, but they do require a commitment to communication and to sharing the values on which relationships are built. Families and communities are built on trust and confidence that have been tested over time, based on an appreciation of shared values that again and again prove more important than mere things. What is vitally important to any society is mutual respect and people's willingness to help each other under any circumstance. Being there for someone else who needs help is a vital part of being human. We demonstrate our competence and trustworthiness with every choice we make. Shared ideas and personal convictions are what humanity, in its best sense, requires.

We don't have to accept the isolation of living in a world void of shared conviction, taught and revered. There is a meaningful, rewarding world out there that we can share with our friends, neighbors, and loved ones. There are such things as moral values that we are capable of identifying and applying to make the most of our lives. Someday our intellectual leaders will stand up and do their jobs. But we have to stop waiting on them.

Young people, if you cannot get honest answers to life's challenges from the adults around you, start your own discussion group. What is at stake is nothing less than your future. Personal convictions, the truth, honesty and integrity matter. Listen to what adults, teachers, and politicians are saying. Words convey ideas; ideas are the building blocks to human success. If we don't stand for something, we will fall for anything.

Blindly following or obeying is not how responsible adults conduct themselves. Solving problems does require some personal courage. Eventually we have to stand up and recognize the fact that we *don't need to live like doormats.* You are not obligated in any way to pay taxes to support senseless wars or corrupt government or socialist programs, including Social Security, Medicare, and Medicaid. You have to demand respect for your rights. Freedom comes with an obligation to exercise personal responsibility and individual initiative. Working Americans are the backbone of this great nation, but working Americans must re-examine the lies and distortions being pushed on them by social engineers. The convoluted spin of America's intellectuals is so calculated, demeaning, and unnecessary that it will go down in history as the greatest failure of this nation.

A country built on history changing ideals, betrayal of those ideals is the only thing that can destroy that country.

We have got to stop acting like a bunch of sheep, following incompetent rulers who clearly have no respect for the principles upon which healthy progress depends. We need to put an end to the system that inflicts pain and suffering and then blames the victims. We wouldn't keep going back to an auto mechanic who cannot fix our car; we shouldn't tolerate these pompous fools who are apparently completely incapable of finding the key to "fixing" America. We are living with a thousand-pound gorilla on our backs because we are blindly following these clowns down a path that leads nowhere. We should lock them all in a big room and not let them out until they agree on what ideals will build a better world. Today, you would be safer in a crisis with a thousand average Americans, who would set about solving problems with human intelligence and determination, than with a hundred intellectuals, who would stand around wondering if anything should be done and finally call for help—which they would expect to be provided and paid for by working Americans. Such blindness and fancy excuses are not funny; it's sad. And it threatens our most cherished aspirations—the future of America.

Young people, your future is being destroyed by Democrats, Republicans, mediocre education, and the nonsense being touted by college professors and talking heads. Today's commentators promote partisan debate (gridlock, shutting down the government, more government spending) while remaining silent about the underlying moral emptiness. This book offers a straightforward discussion of the core values upon which your future ultimately depends.

How much time do you spend considering the kind of person you are? Are you part of the solution, or part of the problem? When was the last time you had a discussion about the values that build a successful nation? Are you confident that we are building a better future for the next generation? Do you view "laws" and "government" as institutions we all must rely on?

In the following pages I will be discussing the core values on which a free and successful society must be built. I have read numerous books on ethics and philosophy and many analyses of our cultural deficiencies, but what they've all lacked are a discussion of any specific cultural expectations we can establish to end political gridlock and growing public apprehension. There is no middle ground or compromise that will save us from the ongoing decline.

In fact, most of those authors predict that the next crisis is imminent. The flaws in our current political ideologies only serve to perpetuate our country's problems. How long before we admit it is not working? How mediocre does our public education have to become before we get serious about what has to change in American society? How many inhumane wars must we endure before our country takes a new diplomatic path?

There is an alternative to standing helpless on the deck of a sinking ship.

Best Behavior

Remember back in grade school, when our teachers told us that we should strive to be on our "best behavior" all the time. That constant reminder made us feel that the kind of people we were and the kind of community we lived in was important. Unfortunately, it was just another con job. I gradually came to realize that it was all part of a deliberate scam. What our teachers failed to do was define what "best behavior" means. Oh, we were told to be nice, get along, avoid fighting, be honest, obey the rules, and do our homework. But starting in the first grade, we were also taught to depend on the government (e.g., public education), presumably because we are so flawed that we cannot trust ourselves to be responsible for our most basic needs.

In other words, whatever it is, *it's not our fault.* There is no personal responsibility. When we have a problem, it's the System that has failed us. It's up to government to care for us.

This contempt for people was and still is deliberate, a matter of educational and social policy. As a result, instead of respecting and relying on our selves and one another, we are taught to rely on rule makers, on a "collective dependency" that we all must serve and obey if any of our nation's problems are to be solved. This educational philosophy is part of a secret plan to keep us all dependent on the powerful who insist on ruling our lives. And the term "best behavior" remains a vague generality.

We don't need to live like mindless consumers, driven only by money and consumption. *Personal character is what we should be focusing on.* Life is about more than having a widescreen television or latest computer. The good news is that life-sustaining values are neither complicated nor difficult to live by. So let's answer the question that any grade school teacher should have answered: What does it mean to be on our "best behavior"? When we strive to be "the best we can be," what does that require of each of us? Or, put another way, if you want to build a better future for your children, what kind of shared expectations must we model and teach?

I welcome those who are seeking a new path; those who want to address the underlying problem of American society; those who seek to explain, validate, demonstrate, and build on the ideals on which everyone's future absolutely depends. We all want to avoid and prevent disasters. Do you want to pursue your happiness? Do you want to be proud of the kind of person you are? Do you want to do the right thing for your loved ones? Most of us would be far more motivated to get up in the morning if we were confident that we had eliminated the possibility of civil and economic collapse.

Let's take off the blinders.

The Sinking Ship: A Nation Living on Fancy Excuses

Lesson 1: The first step in restoring freedom in America is to talk about how citizens manage their lives instead of learning to rely on government and bureaucrats to escape personal responsibility. Freedom means citizens are responsible. Socialism means no one is responsible and everything will be solved by relying on more government.

2 The Solution

Let's take back control instead of living like obedient sheep. We must learn to lead instead of living as servants.

We have to stop living on the backs of our children and grandchildren. Instead of relying on forced obedience, we have to recognize that the kind of people we are is far more important than how well we obey and submit. We can forge a new path for our country, but we must start with the *shared moral values* on which personal, and everyone's, success must be built.

To start the discussion, I am going to define the two core virtues essential to solving problems instead of creating them. Notice that neither of these values relies on rules, legislation, government, force, obedience, or mandatory sacrifices. In fact, a successful society requires exactly the opposite. These virtues represent the light at the end of a very dark tunnel—the personal convictions necessary to live like people, *problem solvers*, instead of *subjects* and *victims* of insidious corruption.

First, it is impossible to be responsible and solve problems without the virtue of *honesty*. Honesty means we do not rely on excuses. It requires that we answer the challenge or question being addressed. It means that every argument we make must facilitate a solution to the problem. What does the pursuit of happiness mean? Does it mean turning our backs on our neighbors, sitting in front of the television, eating junk food, living on welfare, and dumping our trash into the environment? Just spending our time and money in pursuit of goals without any guiding values is a form of blindness which I define as pragmatism. Honesty means we stop faking it and start getting real about how we approach living. The *pursuit of happiness* and the recognition of *inalienable rights* are great, but as a people, our success, happiness, and long-range peace and prosperity must be built upon honesty.

Second, there will be no solution without the virtue of *respect* for everyone. Respect means we all have the right to live without fear of being denied our natural (inherent) rights. That respect for people's right to pursue the best within themselves, is what our Founding Fathers recognized. "Respect" defines how we want to be treated and, therefore, how we must treat everyone. Each of us wants to be seen as a person, a positive influence and contributor to our family and community. When we respect others, we do not resort to lies, fraud, or force to take advantage; in fact, we reject the use of coercion, disrespect, or contempt of innocent people, neighbors and fellow citizens. We have to trust and respect each other by taking responsibility and standing up to the con artists who use spin, fraud, and coercion to intimidate everyone, to keep us all living in fear. It's that respect for individual rights that made America so exceptional—and which has now been erased in modern America.

The Virtue of Honesty

We have all witnessed the consequences of failing to take control of one's life. *Lying* means deceiving someone for ill-gotten gain, for harmless fun, or on occasion, for protection of the innocent. But when dishonesty and faking it become habitual, they undermine the integrity necessary to problem solving. Habitual dishonesty means becoming addicted to bad habits, elaborate excuses, and self-destructive habits. Lying means deceiving oneself through self-deception; ignoring the obvious consequences of our actions, bad habits, and public policies. We've become addicted to a culture built on promises that are propaganda—a free ride, a welfare/warfare system—because we don't want to be honest.

This blindness is perpetuated by our reliance on contrived ideologies and fancy excuses—pragmatism and subjectivism. *Pragmatism* means pursuing our goals while ignoring the unintended consequences of the way we pursue them. Politicians and CEOs love such blindness, as it relieves them of any personal accountability. Spin has replaced honest communication. If you want evidence, just turn on the nightly news. Examples of pragmatism would be texting while driving, banking policies that lead to economic collapse, or constant pollution of our environment.

Subjectivism is what we're practicing when our choices are based on what feels good—for example, having a Big Mac, fries, and a Coke because we love them. Or taking out a home mortgage without having to show we have reliable income. We have been duped into believing our favorite ads and political agendas and obeying the rules without worrying about the consequences. We have become a misguided, mediocre nation that is headed down a slippery slope because we have been degenerated and abused into self-delusional emptiness. We have been brainwashed into believing that personal convictions cannot, and need not, be relied upon to solve the challenges life throws at us. We have bought into the presumption that yes, there are societal problems—poverty, inequality, terrorism, pollution etc.—but *they're not our fault*; they are problems that must be solved by government.

Honest discourse begins with the understanding that there really is such a thing as a moral compass that we can talk about and agree upon. Being objective means that everything we believe and every choice we make is based in reality, and that the principles we revere must be tested, validated, and proven over and over—that we'll accept no excuses or elaborate theories that defy logic and reason.

I know this discussion will be very worrisome to many Americans, particularly adults. Breaking the silence is going to be very discomforting to those who have grown up worshiping pragmatism, subjectivism, religion, social safety nets, bailouts, and subsidies, all justify as morally necessary. But the unintended consequence means living on the backs of our children. Such self-delusional justifications and fancy excuses is destroying our children's future. And television is the government/corporate indoctrination machine that keeps us all ignorant, obedient, and living in fear.

> In short, the first loyalty of many journalists is not to their readers or television audiences who seek information from them but to protecting the image and interests of the groups they represent . . . . Such journalists are also under peer

pressure to filter the news, rather than report the
facts straight.
      Thomas Sowell, *Intellectuals and Society*, 2012

Honesty means, above all else, knowing how to solve
problems by facing reality. Drug abuse, the health-care
crisis, poverty, crime, wars, pollution persist because they
are, at their root, human deficiencies that will be solved
only though personal commitments and expectations.
One illustration of the fog we now endure: you won't find
"personal judgment," "coping with reality," or "solving
problems" as part of the definition of honesty in any
dictionary because the rule makers *do not* want people
exercising judgment, solving problems, or working in
cooperation with one another. That is how they con us
into living like doormats. The 99 percent protestors
don't really bother the elites, because in order to effect
meaningful change, people have to be able to form coherent
convictions, a shared vision. We know what the protestors
were protesting against (the growing disparity between the
rich and the rest of us) but what were they protesting *for*?
People must have a vision on which to build a future or they
are lost, with no understanding of what to do differently.
That is what *honesty* makes possible: it allows us to take
control of our lives and know how to live like problem
solvers dealing with reality. Instead of living like obedient
sheep, dependent on government, we would know how to
live like people who solve problems.

If we cannot be honest and know when we are being
deliberately misled, we won't be able to solve basic
problems. For example, we've been misled into wars and
financial collapse based on fallacious information and
outright lies because we did not demand honest answers;

we simply believed what we were told, without regard for the probable consequences. Here is a definition from my dictionary.

> **Honest** *1. Not lying, cheating, stealing or taking unfair advantage, honorable, truthful, trustworthy. 2. a. Not characterized by deception or fraud; genuine. b. Not calculated or constructed to defraud. 3. Equitable; fair.*

Consider yourself very fortunate if you can you find an adult who can explain what *not lying, cheating, stealing, or taking unfair advantage* means. Look around you. We are living in a culture in which lying, cheating, stealing, and taking unfair advantage are common. Need I remind you that we live in a country that has put ourselves and our children $17 trillion in debt? Such deliberate corruption—and yes, it is deliberate—is an example of systematic deception, *lying, cheating, stealing, or taking unfair advantage*, because such lies and ideologies is what we have been taught to rely on. And there is no plan to reverse this descent into ever-increasing national confusion. If CEOs, politicians, and bankers cannot be honest with the people they serve, what kind of people are they? And what kind of people are we? If they had admitted the truth— *We are going to leave your children trillions of dollars in debt*—would we have elected them? I hope not. But we did elect them, over and over!

The question concerning honesty is this: How do we distinguish valid principles from fraudulent ideologies intended to manipulate us? In discussions of a societal problem, is the most crucial information being provided to us? Is the goal of the media to solve the problem or perpetuate the confusion, the nonsense, and the contempt for people? An answer has to provide the most essential, vital information, or it's a fraud.

The ongoing dishonesty allows those in power to claim almost anything is true, fair, honest, compassionate, equitable, and genuine. Leaving out critical pieces of information is current standard operating procedure. It means "compassion" can mean mandated national health care, and "personal liberty" can mean denying women control over their own bodies. It can mean punishing whistle-blowers for exposing the truth. It allows reliance on subjective and pragmatic excuses to justify almost anything. Modern discourse promotes *looking good* while leading our country into a *catastrophe* (endless wars and growing national debt). Today we're supposed to trust and believe political leaders and professors because they have our best interest at heart. They claim to be dedicated, motivated, loving, uncompromising Americans promoting hope and change. And blindly, we believe them. They use spin to deliberately conceal an authoritarian system and public policies that are inherently self-destructive. The emperors managing the authoritarian state and corrupt financial system have us standing on the deck of a sinking ship because they like the power, prestige, and wealth they gain—at least temporarily.

We must take back control of our lives. We must stop cooperating with and funding the corruption. We must teach and practice a shared set of convictions instead of relying on bad habits, spin, and rule makers. We now live in a mental fog, claiming that we are doing the right thing but never taking the time to define what "right" and "wrong" mean. If we don't make some basic changes, the man-made disasters, the ongoing descent down the slippery slope destroying our country are going to persist.

The solution requires that we teach and abide by a moral compass that is specific, real, tangible, valid, and motivating because it solves our problems. Then our children will have the knowledge on how to grow up and become the best they can be.

Mushy definitions will no longer be tolerated. To be honest we must define and justify every concept we trust and rely upon. There is no shortcut, free ride, promised land, or divine rule maker. We cannot create wealth, or a strong economy, by printing money. We cannot be honest only when it's convenient. We cannot exercise honest judgment by remaining silent and obedient in the face of corruption. Everything we believe and every choice we make has to reflect our integrity. Honesty is a personal value, a commitment to oneself. The virtue of honesty is what makes us thinking, responsible adults. Every piece of knowledge and every argument we use should first and foremost facilitate healthy choices applicable to the challenge at hand.

But being honest requires more than just coping with reality. People solve problems every day. People make healthy choices 90 percent of the time. What they are not doing is defining how they judge their goals, ideals, values, and convictions and the results, or consequences, of their actions. We are failing as a country because we have no shared moral compass with which to judge our solutions, actions, or goals. We pollute the environment because we enjoy an energy-wasting lifestyle. We have perfected the art of concealing the truth, of remaining silent while we deceive ourselves and everyone else. We live in a mental fog because we like going shopping and watching entertainment that promotes violence, self-destructive behaviors, a world of financial bubbles. So let's begin by being honest.

Honesty means taking responsibility for everything you say and do. When you're reading a book or listening to a professor, you must understand the underlying values, concepts, and solutions being recommended. Are the authors and commentators basing their views on logic and reason or on delusional fantasies? When you pick up a dictionary, for example, do you expect the authors to provide valid definitions. Do you judge for yourself of just accept whatever is being promoted? When you vote and pay taxes, do you assume the tax money will be spent to uphold everyone's rights and liberties. Or, is the kind of governing we endure our responsibility? When you tolerate politicians who get elected with false promises, you are part of the underlying cause of societal injustice.

Once you start to understand what honesty means, you will be able to detect dishonesty in everyday life. You will learn to recognize the fraudulent in every argument and ideology you encounter. You will be able to distinguish integrity from fraud and corruption in just a few sentences. This new power of discernment will give your life a whole new meaning and build your confidence in others and yourself. We will be able to recognize deceivers and con artists. We will resolutely reject the gullibility that has rendered us helpless slaves, doormats, and peons. We will stop depending on government bureaucrats, bailouts, and handouts. We will start demanding integrity from ourselves and those around us. In a relatively short time, we will be living in a whole new world, a world where we all are expected to take responsibility for everything we say and do.

This is not rocket science, but it does require that each of us examines what kind of person we are and what kind of people we should become. Starting at age six, we should be prepared to talk to one another and validate every choice we make. That is what *being on our best behavior* means. To function as adults, we must work together by defining our shared responsibilities, goals, expectations, and compassions: *love of life* and the *pursuit of happiness* based on our highest expectations—with no excuses.

The meaning of "honesty":

- ☐ that we take responsibility for everything we say and do
- ☐ that which is validated by, and consistent with, reality
- ☐ providing the essential information for every challenge, question, and problem
- ☐ talking about "right" and "wrong," and those contrived ideologies that result in human suffering

The Virtue of Respect

Respect for one another is the other painted line or guardrail necessary to keep us on the road to success. And just like the virtue of honesty, respect is an elementary concept, easy to understand and apply to our everyday lives. And just like honesty, respect is largely ignored and twisted today to keep us helpless and subservient. The concept of respect clearly addresses how we want to be treated and how we should treat one another. Unfortunately, this essential virtue suffers from the same ongoing mushy thinking. Here is some of the mushy confusion from my dictionary, The American Heritage Dictionary.

> ***Respect*** *1. To feel or show esteem for; to honor. 2. To show consideration for; avoid violation of; treat with deference. 3. To relate or refer to.*

Modern dictionary definitions reveal the mental fog used to keep everything malleable and uncertain about personal qualities of character. So, as a breath of fresh air, let's clearly define the terms by which we should get along with one another—what kind of expectations we should hold for ourselves when dealing with our fellow citizens. Being honest means defining our terms in order to make healthy choices and protect ourselves from con artists. So what does "respect" require of each of us?

We all want to live in a community where we can benefit from our efforts and accomplishments without fear of being assaulted, robbed, or molested. When in a room full of people, we would absolutely not pick the pockets of other people, and they, in turn, would not pick our pockets. In other words, respect means we do not rob, steal, and plunder or resort to fraud, intimidation, or negligence to get ahead or take advantage. If someone dropped his wallet, or her purse, we would pick it up and return it to him or her. But respect means more than just being considerate of the people around us. Respect means trusting everyone to take our shared principles seriously because all people deserve the same opportunity in life—to live confident that their efforts and accomplishments are theirs to use or share.

Respect means communicating with people because we value life and the rewards made possible by living a noble life. It means wanting what is best for everyone and recognizing that we have to cooperate and work together. Just as we must preserve the natural environment, we must preserve and stand up for humanity, justice, fairness and respect for everyone's rights.

What went wrong? We live in a country built on the highest standards, promising that we can lead healthy and productive lives and not rob and assault one another. We celebrate our commitment to personal values, and then voters elect politicians to manage a government whose primary function is to pick the pockets of every American—to rob, steal, plunder, and intimidate. Talk about cultural bankruptcy! We embrace taxes, welfare programs, regulations, bureaucrats, intimidation, and foreign interventions that contradict the principles we claim to revere. Today every problem is solved through public policies, police, government, coercion, legislation, and social mandates. Every problem is expected to be solved through collective regimentation. What nonsense. The focus on respect, personal expectations, and responsibility that is essential to behaving like an adult has become a joke in America.

The Founding Fathers established a government that was intended to protect people, not threaten them. Today, in stark contrast, we're told (promised) that government is going to solve all our problems. The very idea of people having control and responsibility no longer exists in our culture. The flaw in our culture today is the abandonment of the principle set forth in our Constitution that each of us has an *inalienable right to life, liberty, and the pursuit of happiness.* The notion that government should provide for people's retirement, health care, education, and financial aid (including subsidies and loop-holes for businesses and corporations) is exactly the opposite of the spirit of respect and voluntary cooperation upon which a healthy nation must be built. Force and intimidation are not how people solve problems and face challenges. Respecting each other means we live the way nature intended, like rational beings and not like bullies and parasites. Anyone claiming we can address growing societal disparity relying on government while ignoring our underlying moral emptiness is part of the ongoing problem.

Today we treat people like dolts, assuming they are so inherently incompetent and untrustworthy that they must live (for the good of the nation, of course) enslaved to the dictates of benevolent rulers (the military/financial/corporate/nanny-state complex). Simply stated, we live in the one country dedicated to personal liberty and have now abandoned any commitment and regard for that ideal. Our government is viewed not as the protector of our rights but as the authority everyone must obey.

Respect means not robbing, stealing, and intimidating others, and not cooperating with those who abuse and ignore people's rights. It's a pretty elementary concept, but you will not find such a definition printed in our dictionaries or taught in our schools or practiced by our legal system. What our society teaches is that we should rob our neighbors to provide for everybody's needs, globalize our military, hand out corporate subsidies and bailouts, and that such mandatory sacrifices are morally justified.

Our growing national debt and oppressive taxes are evidence that we don't have any shared convictions about how to respect one another. Are you paying attention? Go online and Google government taxes and spending. Taxes now consume more than half the average American family's budget ($41,000 per household in 2011), and federal government spending represents 25 percent of the gross domestic product. If we returned to legitimate, constitutional government (and taxes to support legitimate government), the take-home pay of the average family would increase by about $30,000 per year. Could families better afford basic necessities, food, health care, and education with $30,000 more of their hard-earned money? We will recover that money, and get the thousand-pound gorilla off our backs, only when we choose to stop living dependent on compulsory extortion, militarism, subsidies, and fancy excuses.

We are the problem. We like living on the backs of future generations. We like a free ride where government (or the FED) prints all the money we need. We have embraced contempt for people instead of with respect for people and the integrity that people should stand for. We live in a country that celebrates its love of freedom and then, on a daily basis, acts in a way that reflects exactly the opposite philosophy (ideologies)—that enslaves everyone. We, the leaders of the free world, apparently will not practice what we preach.

The meaning of "respect":

□ recognizing the right of each to their life, liberty and pursuit of happiness
□ treating everyone equally and fairly
□ not tolerating the use of fraud, force, intimidation or deception to take advantage of anyone
□ using force only in self-defense
□ insisting on government that sets forth a legal system to protect its citizens, not to enslave them

- □ making self-realization and self-control part of your moral compass
- □ do not pollute or poison the environment

Welcome to the New World

As you read this book, you'll be expected to judge every example and evaluate how you would answer every question and challenge being discussed. That is your responsibility.

As an example of our ability to exercise integrity, participate in the discussion and formulation of valid arguments, evaluate the following quotation for its honesty. This is one example of the world we now inhabit—one of habitual, delusional nonsense. It's just one small example to illustrate the importance of being honest with ourselves and one another. Yes, you are now taking that first step into a new world, a world where we demand to know and understand everything that impacts people's lives. A new day is coming when we will evaluate, test, validate, talk about, and take responsibility, because that is what being on our "best behavior" requires. Here is a quotation from US Supreme Court Chief Justice John Roberts, discussing the Supreme Court's 2012 ruling on the constitutionality of national (federal) health-care legislation:

> We do not consider whether the act embodied sound policies. That judgment is entrusted to the nation's elected leaders. We ask only whether Congress has the power under the Constitution to enact the challenged provisions.

When I read this quote online, after I stopped laughing, I copied it down. At the time there was a lot of commentary about this court ruling (the debate is still going on), but clearly something was missing: an honest discussion of the essential questions being raised by this Supreme Court challenge and ruling.

The debate over national health care is just another example of how this nation cannot reach agreement on anything. There's a lot of talk without substance, and plenty of convoluted arguments, but there's no honest debate or recognition of how to address the problems in our health-care system. We endure endless debates and court rulings over what is supposedly "constitutional" but there is no solution or agreement, just endless debate and grid lock.

This quote sounds like the chief justice is defining the role of the court. Each branch of government serves a specific role in upholding the Constitution and protecting our liberties. Should the Supreme Court's role be to verify the constitutionality of the laws passed and the methods used in enforcing those laws? If not, what is the purpose of having a Supreme Court or a legal system to protect our rights and liberties? What does protecting our rights and liberties mean?

Now read the above quotation again. Does the chief justice clearly define and explain the basis for the court's ruling? Does he recognize the role of government, legislation, or the law in our society? Judging from his quote, the Supreme Court need discern only whether Congress has the power under the Constitution to enact the challenged provisions. Apparently, it has no responsibility to judge the legitimacy or constitutionality of legislation. Apparently, the constitutionality or intent of laws is of no concern to the courts. It need consider only whether Congress has the power and authority to enact legislation. If Congress passed legislation requiring everyone to vote and mandated that nonvoters pay a fine, apparently that law would be acceptable to the Supreme Court. If elected representatives enact any law through the "legislative process," according to the Chief Justice, the law is constitutional. There are apparently *no principles* that the Constitution stands for. That's right— this is just more evidence of the rationalizations used to deceive the public. Under the current system, the courts and the American people need not consider whether the law *embodied sound policies*; apparently, sound policies based on valid convictions are of no concern. Those revered principles (whatever they are) do not matter or are not definable. The absence of any agreement about our shared values means endless debate, confusion, and gridlock. We're trying to sound dedicated, intelligent, and compassionate while recognizing nothing as certain. This means there are no principles embodied within the US Constitution that the courts or the public need to define and practice. This is why we now live as obedient subjects of government instead of holding high expectations for ourselves and our elected leaders.

In modern America it's not because there are no principles. It's because we refuse to talk about or recognize the need to define those principles. It would be like playing a game of basket ball but never agreeing on the rule of the game. The results would be, and clearly are, chaos.

What if elected representatives enacted legislation requiring citizens to pay for their own health care? Would the courts rule such legislation unconstitutional? Who knows what principles, if any, they actually espouse. Today, no one is expected to explain himself or justify how he conducts his life. We tolerate mandated, collective obligations or going it alone because we won't discuss what kind of people or nation we are (or should be). The endless debates never get to the essential questions. Yet, how we should get along with one another is no more complicated than the rules of a basket ball game.

So, being honest, let's answer the question: Is government-funded health care constitutional? The answer is no, because each of us has an inalienable right to our lives, to the money we earn, and should not be forced to pay for anyone's health care. Under our Constitution, the government has no authority to enslave its citizens. The government as set forth by our Constitution is supposed to protect people, not make them servants of the collective. In a free society, where people respect one another, we promote the collective good my recognizing and respecting the rights of everyone. If we don't recognize the rights of everyone then, ultimately, we live in fear of our government.

It remains the responsibility of the courts, juries, and citizens to *evaluate and judge* the validity and constitutionality of *everything* our government does. That is what personal integrity and a shared moral compass require. It should come as no surprise that during the nomination and approval process to serve on the nation's highest court, Supreme Court candidates are never asked to define the principles this nation and Constitution stand proudly for. The meaning and purpose of the "law" that guides the nation are never discussed, defined, or articulated. And those concepts are not taught in our law schools, either. This institutional silence allows the emperors to indulge in perpetual corruption. We now endure a legal system so confused and unprincipled it has become a threat to us all. And, it's no accident—the confusion is deliberate because it allows the "rulers" to get away with almost anything.

Constitutional principles are not complicated. Before we reach age ten, we should begin learning to stand up for our individual rights and take personal responsibility for our actions. We have to define our societal values for the same reason that we should define every concept and word we use. The purpose of the law is to protect the rights of citizens to manage their own lives, not to render everyone obedient servants of government. When the courts, legislators, and voters insist that health care is a legitimate government service, then—being *honest*—we know what kind of culture we will endure: one of institutional servitude, where we live like peons and oppressed taxpayers. But *institutional servitude* is not what America is supposed to represent. Servitude is not inherent to human nature, and when we remain silent on the issue, we're guilty of criminal complicity. And guess what? Most of us know that: We are the problem. Welcome to America, where deliberately delusional thinking and habitual dishonesty are destroying our culture and our children's future.

Honesty is like a breath of fresh air. It's like turning the lights on. It is motivating, inspiring, and life-sustaining. Honesty in society means we all take responsibility for the choices we make every day: you and I, our friends and neighbors, teachers and commentators. You may notice a concept there that you have never heard before: our standards for personal character should be the same for *everyone* and applicable to *every challenge* we face. There is no prospect of building *humanity* without *shared values*. Different people don't live in different realities. Right and wrong are not indefinable concepts. The Constitution is not supposed to be malleable, serving the special interests of whoever is in office. When we allow our government to treat citizens like servants, we have little or no respect for ourselves or our neighbors. Thus we live like doormats, pawns of lobbyists, politicians, and the well connected.

If people refuse to sit down and agree on the principles the nation stands for, then at the very least they should wear lapel pins stating, *I cannot be trusted.* Working together to solve problems is entirely within the realm of our potential and our responsibility as individuals and a community. Without a set of shared convictions, we are left standing alone, relying on rulers who make excuses, recognize no shared convictions, and kick the can down the road. To stop kicking the can down the road we will have to agree on what principles and ideals are necessary to solve our problems.

What if we made it our business to define right from wrong? Then we could work together, and understand, agree upon, and expect from everyone his or her "best behavior." What an inspiration! Such systemic honesty is not new. We all engage in financial transactions because we are honest about the mathematics that makes managing our money and doing business possible. We all drive on the same side of the road because we all agree that doing so makes us 100 percent safer. Now consider our constitutional commitment to the right of each person to *life, liberty, and the pursuit of happiness.* There is no national discussion or recognized need for commitment to any shared expectations about how to live like responsible adults.

The growing apprehension among Americans tells us how well we are facing the trials and tribulation life throws at us. Our sense of confidence tells us whether we have learned and applied the values and ideals by which we should be living. Our successes, accomplishments, and personal security are the result—the judge and jury of our moral choices. When we feel the need for security guards, install security systems in our homes or live in gated communities, it's because we have failed to live like adults, with respect for other people based on a set of shared convictions. Whether or not we admit it, we judge ourselves and each other, and we know when we are failing. We are punished or rewarded for our choices, not only by our material successes, but also by the joys and failures of living a good and noble life. That is why art, music, poetry, love, friends, pride, and recognition of character all are more important than material possessions. But all those things are products of personal initiative and shared expectations—not caprice, luck, blind obedience, excuses, or social scientists pulling strings and legislating rules everyone must obey. It is institutionalized obedience that now poisons our culture and undermines our confidence. And it is the absence of any shared convictions, such as *honesty* and *respect*, leaves us helpless to solve the challenges that we now face as a nation and individuals.

Some Examples

To illustrate what *honesty* and *respect* mean, let's examine a couple of current hot-button issues—Social Security and gay marriage. I understand that many adults are not going to like this discussion because there're convinced that some "authority" should define and decide these issues for us. They are convinced that people cannot, and should not, judge these things for themselves. However, there is some evidence that today's youth are beginning to realize how moral issues like these deserve our attention. There is growing evidence that some of us are beginning to reach agreement that we need to talk about such issues and that there is such a thing as a vision, a explicit meaning to "right" and "wrong".

Do social safety nets designed to provide for the poor and elderly demonstrate morality? Is defining marriage as between one man and one woman a proper role for government? Whose role it is to promote moral behavior and strong families? If we decide it is "government" that should decide these issues and impose these obligations and standards, then *what does personal responsibility mean?* Does personal responsibility mean mandatory obedience or shared values to judge and decide how each should live their lives?

Lack of trust, convictions, and expectations makes people "problems" to be cared for instead of "problem solvers" who know how to address and provide for their own needs. If we embrace welfare programs on a massive scale, we have not demonstrated respect or honesty or compassion—we have simply created institutionalized servitude. America does not stand for institutionalized servitude. Social safety nets are not solutions; they are oppressive regulations that rob people of their rights, and the shared expectations on which civilization must be built. Such imposed obedience and dependency ultimately makes matters worse. In a *free society*, people work together voluntarily to address the suffering of the sick, and homeless. Persistent social ills, are addressed through shared expectations, self-realization, problem solving, earning a living, and voluntary cooperation—and most important, *teaching and revering the personal values upon which individual success must be built.* In a healthy society we teach people how to solve problems instead of how to make excuses. In a free society we *care* about everyone but we *do not* enslave anyone. And because we care about one another, we talk about what matters most; what kind of people we are; the convictions, values, and expectations we must live by in order to address the challenges life throws at us.

Marriage is a personal choice, not an edict handed down by politicians. To allow some judge, religious guru, or legislator to define our personal relationships means we have decided that we are too incompetent to manage our most private choices. It is the responsibility of each of us to respect the individual's right to decide what kind of loving relationship he or she wants. How we conduct our personal lives is our own responsibility. The question is, how are we to raise our families if we turn off our brains and live obedient to legislators? Mandated obedience does not represent respect or justice or morality. It represents bullying by adults who refuse to acknowledge the need to exercise responsibility and respect the rights and abilities of others. If people are presumed incapable of exercising personal responsibility in their most personal choices, *freedom* and *moral responsibility* become meaningless concepts. That reliance on force to subvert citizens' rights and responsibility is the elephant in America's living room, and the bullying only grows worse.

People of character do not pay oppressive taxes, participate in needless wars, run up massive debts, and tolerate all sorts of violations of people's rights and then claim to value individual liberty. Turn off the television. Put down the cell phone. The personal convictions and ideals that America represents must start in our homes, around the dining room table. Want to live in an entirely different kind of world? Want to live in a free society with respect for everyone? What are we waiting for?

Lesson 2: There is no alternative: everything we do must be based on our determination to solve problems rather than making excuses and making matters worse. We have a choice: act like bullies, or acting with personal integrity—doing the right thing—as how people of character build enduring confidence, peace, and prosperity.

3 Wake Up, America

The Truth—using honest evaluation to address and solve society's problems is not difficult. Learning to treat everyone with respect is not difficult. A nation that does not teach and revere these essential values is a nation running on empty.

Evidence of our country's pervasive blindness first revealed itself to me when I was in the first grade. One day my teacher, whom we students had come to admire, stood up in front of the class wearing a very stern, emotionless expression, and students knew we were about to be told something very important. When the room was dead silent, our teacher said, "If any student skips class, we will send the truancy officer after you." As first graders, we didn't understand the implications of such a policy. It took years for me to comprehend that we were being taught not how to live like competent adults (people with respect for one another) but how to live like *obedient cogs in an authoritarian machine*. We were being taught to depend on government. Instead of learning the importance of *honesty* and *respect*, we were taught to rely on *legislation* and *obedience*. And we were supposed to cooperate because such obedience was what was *good* and *best* for all of us. In fact, such obedience represented the "worst behavior" in terms of what we should expect of ourselves. The meaning of "best behavior" was never discussed; that would have meant recognizing our need for self-expectations, self-realization, self-control, and coherent explanations. We were being raised, educated not to live as competent citizens, but as obedience sheep.

After her announcement, my first-grade teacher then returned to her usual friendly demeanor and we all relaxed again. We all relaxed to be subjected to a mediocre education—to the indoctrination and brainwashing that deliberately omits the qualities of character essential to making the most of our lives, and living in a society built on voluntary cooperation. (For more on this subject, the refusal to teach moral values, read *Save the World on Your Own Time* by Stanley Fisk.)

I recently heard a news report about a Texas honor student who worked part-time jobs to support her two siblings and was ordered to spend twenty-four hours in jail and pay a hundred-dollar fine after she missed a few days of school. This is an example of how we treat students—like subjects who must conform, submit, and live obedient and complacent.

This honor student deserved our support and admiration instead of jail time. Stories like this are just more evidence that the professions that are failing America are the police and legal profession, which is supposed to protect citizens, and educators who are supposed to teach qualities of character.

I grew up in "the land of opportunity." I now live in an America that feels more like a very large prison with little light, no windows, and a putrid cloud of smoke so that no one has to talk to anyone he or she comes in contact with. It's a world where people drive around in race cars with tinted windows so they never have to look at or be looked at by anyone. It's a nation where you can walk down the sidewalk and no one will look at you or smile. Have you noticed the pickup trucks with extra-large exhaust pipes that make a loud noise when the driver accelerates, as if he wants to show how proud he is that he can annoy people on the road around him and pollute the air they are breathing?

The message: every choice a person makes is a reflection of their humanity or lack of humanity, their values or lack of values, their qualities of character or lack thereof. Taking responsibility for everything we say and do is not just some empty slogan. It means being a source of the human potential, or being a hazard to one's self and everyone else. And making that choice is the difference between living in pursuit of the best within us instead of living as a burden on society. Every choice we make is a reflection of what kind of person we choose to be—a problem solver or a burden.

Here in Denver there was a recent proposal to charge a five-cent fee for every plastic bag used by shoppers at grocery stores. The advocates of this fee like it because it would reduce the amount of plastic dumped into the environment. Freedom advocates, in contrast, hated the fee because it's just another tax on working Americans. Both are half-right. The problem is the absence of an honest argument about societal values. In a healthy society, we wouldn't need such meddlesome laws because everyone would take responsibility for the way they live and their impact on the environment. On a windy day in Colorado, you can see sagebrush blowing across the roads and fields, but you can also see plastic bags blowing across the roads and fields and hung up in trees and on fences. People just turn a blind eye to the consequences of the choices they make and their impact on other people and on the environment. And, when things get so out of control or problems grow too burdensome we are taught that the solution is to resort to government and more legislation. And opposing such fees and regulation without addressing the moral emptiness is also not a solution. Only responsible adults can make a society work successfully.

I was one of those demoralized and frustrated students, so when I was required to take some elective courses to graduate from college, I signed up for *Ethics 101* to see if I could discover the source of my confusion. During the first few classes, some of the students (who had more courage than I) pressed the professor to answer a simple question: What moral principles will you be teaching and recommending? Sounds like a fairly basic question. Talking about what had gone wrong in America was on the minds of students clear back on the 60s.

His response, which was slow in coming, was both revealing and demoralizing. He would not be recommending any specific values, principles, or moral standards. Apparently he agreed with the opinion that any set of values, or even no values at all, represents modern morality, and that professors have no responsibility for teaching students how to make healthy choices. It should come as no surprise that we students didn't show much interest in the materials being taught, and the professor didn't show much interest in us students. That's what modern education has denigrated into, it's called mediocre education.

Let's talk about what life in a free society would look and feel like, and the shared qualities that would make such a society work. Perhaps this is the first time you have heard or read a discussion like this. Certainly, I rarely heard the subject discussed when I was growing up.

In American history there are numerous examples of trying to solve problems with more government: the War on Drugs, the civil rights movement, the War on Poverty, and No Child Left Behind legislation. The results are notable for their mediocre results.

Here is an example of how a shared moral compass would make all the difference. Here is an example of a society that does not rely on government, but relies on personal convictions. Here is what living a free society must teach and require of its citizens.

The CEO of a very large banking institution, he manages the mortgage division, walks into his office stops at his secretary's desk to get his agenda for the day. His secretary, who has been working with him for years, hands him the schedule, saying, "We received a memorandum that I put on your desk."

The CEO goes into his office and reads the memorandum, a proposal on new lending policies to increase the bank's profitability. It recommends that the bank offer to its customers, mortgages with no proof of earning or income, no money down, and artificially low adjustable rates. The loans would be guaranteed through two new federal lending institutions, Fannie May and Freddie Mac.

After reading the memo, the CEO calls his secretary into his office and says, "Get me a list of all those who prepared these proposed lending policies."

She replies, "I am already working on it. They are all going to be fired, aren't they?"

The CEO responds, "Once people embrace contrived excuses, re-educating them becomes very problematic. I hired these executives because I trusted them. I didn't hire them to scam our customers. It is my job to manage the mortgage division of this vitally important banking institution. If these lending incentives and government guarantees became standard policies, they would eventually bring down the whole banking system. I will not be part of such corruption."

For lack of such values and integrity we were led into the financial collapse of 2008, and we've been told over and over that the solution to the problem is government regulation of banks. In fact, the problem is a lack of shared personal convictions. Moral values, shared and practiced by everyone is how a healthy society looks, feels, and acts. Citizens, including its corporate leaders, would not tolerate corruption and organized shenanigans. There is no alternative; that is how a free society must function if we are to sustain human progress.

A married couple goes to their bank to apply for a home mortgage. "You've come at the right time," the mortgage advisor tells them. "You can get a mortgage with no proof of earning, no money down, at a low adjustable rate, and the government will guarantee it if you default." These responsible people look at each other, laugh out loud, and get up and leave. They know a fraud when they see one; they know that financial institutions that gamble with their customers' money and encourage their customers to play the system are nothing but casinos. Within two weeks they have closed all their accounts with the bank and have moved to a different, locally owned bank that promises to exercise basic integrity.

These responsible adults feel sorry for people who have been indoctrinated into relying on such schemes, but they act on their convictions and take the necessary steps to protect their family. That is the difference between those who live on fancy excuses, trusting in the corrupt system, verses those who recognize the need for meaningful convictions and taking responsibility for their finances, their personal welfare, and their families.

These examples illustrate not only what has to change for our country to succeed again, but also how easy such changes will be once people learn what *best behavior* and *being adults* mean and require of them.

That is how a free society must function to achieve the lasting financial security that we should expect. Prior to the 2008 financial collapse, did you hear one financial expert (from the left or right ideologies) warn us about the coming collapse? Did you hear anyone warn homebuyers about the scams they were being led into by the banks and government financial services? What does such silence and shenanigans tell us about our culture? Yet we are told over and over that more government is the only solution. We were not told about this pending collapse because those who claim to be serving society don't what citizens to know what scams they are perpetrating. This collapse was not an accident, a result of poor judgment—it was the result of moral emptiness.

Yet every financial lobbyist in Washington knew, without being told, that a major taxpayer bailout of the savings and loan industry was in the works for 1989. They began to lay the groundwork for it early by drafting their own self-interested blueprints for how the next president should solve the problem. Distant from the empty politics of presidential campaigns, these bailouts proposals were circulating freely among key political players.

John H. Zaugg

William Greider, *Who Will Tell the People: The Betrayal of American Democracy,* 1992

Bailouts of lending institutions and banks started in 1990, but the real collapse and betrayal came in 2008 from which we are still recovering. The ensuing recessing was a result of trusting in elites to exercise some basic integrity. In fact they are the emperors up on stage, wearing fancy clothes made of invisible thread. Their real mission is to formulate the system to grow every more powerful and rich.

In a free society, banks would be private, locally owned institutions with no government regulations. Instead of allowing government to regulate our mortgages, business, and banks, we would insist upon government that holds people and businesses accountable if they commit fraud, theft, or harm to others, either deliberately or through schemes to rob working citizens. There is a basic difference between bureaucratic regulators which impose rules, and the "rule of law" that protects citizens from criminal conduct and schemes by holding accountable those perpetrating such crimes. Claiming we desperately need such rules creates the oppressive, meddlesome bureaucracy, and false promises, that citizens and taxpayers endure. Under the rule of law, such contrived burdens, corruption, and taxes would never be allowed. The two goals of a moral compass would be *fairness* and *justice.* Citizens would not tolerate government redistribution of wealth because such taxes results in what may be described as organized crime, and would hold those accountable who benefit from the corruption. When we buy into the scam that government policies and agencies should manage the economy, we are setting ourselves (working citizens) up to bail out banks and corporations when they fail. Economic prosperity depends on how well people manage their own earnings, finances and money. Turning such responsibilities over to government is how the emperors perpetuate their schemes and legislated economic policies.

The bad news is the elites, politicians and scam artists are leading us into another economic collapse. By not being able to pay for all the promises benevolent government has made, to both citizens and business interests, we are faced with another fiscal cliff. The problem is, this time the government and the FED are so in-debt and over-extended that there is no back room deal to bailout or save the economy from bankruptcy. The whole system is going to go into permanent recession until someone stands up and begin to teach and rebuild the house on the hill based on a foundation of moral principles. The poverty rate and disparity between the haves and have-nots will grow worse until citizens take responsibility for their families, money, and values on which humanity and prosperity must be built. Simply stated, we have to stop playing the system, living as mindless consumers and start to face reality with convictions that make us the problem solvers instead losers playing in a fancy casino.

Lesson 3: There is no solution relying on force, bureaucrats and rules. The solution requires personal convictions that we rely on to solve problems. Such convictions are the foundation for building the *castle on the hill*. Today we are lied to so consistently that the lies might be described as institutional delusional thinking used to justify living like parasites on the backs of our children.

John H. Zaugg

Any set of rules, bureaucracy, and taxes to fund legislated management of people's lives and businesses (e.g. War on Drugs, Government run health care, Social Security, subsidies, corporate bailouts, and Home Land Security that violate citizens rights and liberties) are evidence of the moral emptiness.

4 Thanksgiving 1823

Those who deny freedom to others deserve it not for themselves.
Abraham Lincoln, 1809-65

A documentary I watched on television offered an excellent example of the choice we are making as a community. It illustrated the choice that people make that determines their long range success. I don't remember what network the show was on and didn't get to watch all of it, so I can't give credit where credit is due. But the message it illustrated was clear.

The program started with a group of natives meeting in their local forest, a natural resource their village relied upon. They were meeting to discuss, talk about and reach agreement about, which trees they would cut down and how to best sustain the forest for the long term. Then the documentary presented another meeting, this one of government officials who were discussing the logistics of allowing foreign corporations to come into the forest and extract natural resources. In the process, the extraction would likely pollute the forest and much of the natural habitat.

The first meeting is an example of how people can talk about preserving what is most vital to their long-range welfare. It illustrates what I call a *shared moral compass.*

The second meeting represents just the opposite. The government and corporate officials deliberately avoided talking to anyone who might stand in the way of their plans to make money. This example illustrates the quest for wealth with no moral values—pragmatism, a deliberate disregard for people, the natural environment, and future generations.

In his book *Collapse: How Societies Choose to Fail or Succeed,* Jared Diamond addresses the subject of why some communities thrived for thousands of years, while others last only a few hundred years, and asks readers to evaluate what is now happening to America. For example, he examines how over the last century, Montana has changed from a free market state with industrial growth into a "welfare state." For every federal tax dollar a Montanan pays the federal government, the state gets in return a $1.50 of taxpayer money—a public expense deemed necessary to save the state from environmental and economic collapse. That collapse was caused by mindless decisions made in the mining, lumber, and agriculture industries over the past hundred years. The question is, are we, the other forty-nine states, going down the same path? The potential collapse in Montana is evidence that its people didn't care to examine what would be required for the long-range success of their state.

What's interesting about Diamond's book is that it addresses the crisis that we, and everyone, are now faced with. He talks about the need for values that must guide our behavior. He concludes with the following assessment of the communities he's studied:

> Two types of choices seem to me to have been
> crucial in tipping their outcomes towards success
> or failure: long-term planning, and willingness to
> reconsider those core values.

What is so mind-boggling (or typical) is the author never addresses or discusses those "core values." But, this is the subject and discussion we need to have. What if, like those natives, the citizens of Montana had talked about ensuring their long-range success? Can we make healthy choices about how we conduct our lives and businesses? Does our success or failure depend on long-term planning and core values? Those are the questions Jared Diamond asks the reader to consider.

Here a story to illustrate what happens when people refuse to be honest about the kind of choices they are making. Here is how living in a community that will not define those core values will look and feel like. Here is an example of how long-term planning and the core values guiding humanity are vitally important to all of us.

Imagine the Thanksgiving ceremonies back in 1823, which brought together some Native Americans and some of the men who fought in the Revolutionary War to win our freedoms and liberties. They spent a day cooking, eating, and talking; it was a great opportunity for them to sit down and talk with their neighbors. Toward the end of the day they were sitting around a campfire when a woman named Kesustra, a teacher at the nearby Indian village, was joined by one of her students, an eleven-year-old. A colonel from the volunteer army was going on about how they had finally defeated and outsmarted the English army—the strongest military force in the world at that time. The eleven-year-old saw his opening and asked the colonel a question:

"Why is it that after such a struggle to secure your rights and liberties, and document the right of each to their life, liberty, and pursuit of happiness, do you insist on forcing natives who have lived here for hundreds of years off their lands and onto reservations hundreds of miles from home? Why do you import natives from Africa to live as slaves? Why do you treat some people with such contempt and then, the next day, preach your mandate to "love thy neighbor"? How do you define "neighbor"? Am I your neighbor? This is a celebration of your historic accomplishment to explicitly recognize the rights of all citizens, but then you deny those rights to those who should be your neighbors."

The eleven-year-old never got an answer.

Kesustra tried to restore the conversation. She looked into the eyes of the colonel and said,

"You and your neighbors and children may attend my school. We make it a priority to teach what competent behavior means and requires. We define what "neighbor" means and how it applies to everyone. We talk about those ideals that make the prospects for enduring peace and prosperity possible. We talk about how we must all share in the struggle to build a better world. What my students and I see happening does not bode well for the future."

She got no response, either.

By 1837, forty-six thousand Native Americans from the southeastern states had been forcibly relocated from their homelands. (To learn more, read *A Century of Dishonor* by Helen Jackson.)

The next time you join in a Thanksgiving celebration, take the opportunity to start a conversation about what matters most to your and everyone's future—long-term planning and core values. If we remain silent or complacent, then we are going down the same path as every other empire in human history—one that ends in failure. We can be a civilization that lasts more than a thousand years, or we can be led into collapse within the next hundred years.

Years ago I was reading the history of the Lewis and Clark expedition (1804-06). What I found amazing is that the explorers came across a Native American tribe that would not retaliate after being attacked or assaulted by others, natives or whites. (This may have been one of many such tribes.) War, murder, and terrorist-type revenge apparently were activities they simply would not engage in. They didn't rely on force to solve their problems; they spent their time and energy focused on the things their survival depended upon, and they survived for hundreds of years. They made how they worked together their core value, instead of relying of force used against anyone.

America is faced with the same challenge. We have the strongest military in the world, but if we collapse into financial bankruptcy, all the military spending may turn out to have been part of the causes of the collapse. Again, it's how we manage our long range endeavors that matters. It's those core values that give us the insight and strength to make healthy choices. Just like those native Indians, I look forward to the day when Christians, Muslims, and Jews can act with the same kind of conviction to choose peace instead of war, drone attacks, torture, and suicide bombings.

The War on Terrorism may appeal to the military, corporate complex, but restoring America may come down to how we forge a path to enduring peace and prosperity that appeals to people's hearts and minds here and around the globe.

Kesustra was right: what's happening does not bode well for the future. The civil war in Syria, the military oppression in Egypt, and the civil unrest around the globe are a result of the failure of government officials and citizens to recognize an alternative to brute force and violence. Further evidence of the underlying problem is that those watching this travesty have no clue what to recommend or do differently. Today we resort to guns, bombs, drone attacks, and civil wars in these situations because people refuse to address the underlying problem. Spending billions of tax dollars on wars, subsidies to foreign dictators, and rebuilding cities we have destroyed means we are sacrificing innocent lives, making more enemies who hate us, and going bankrupt. There is an alternative.

Instead of relying on force, intimidation, bombs, and violence, (funding the military, corporate complex) we need to stand for something that works. Instead of sending armies to invade and overthrow governments and dictators, we need to calm our military obsession and send out peace advocates. These peace advocates would carry no guns; they would simply go into a foreign country, shake hands with its citizens, learn about their culture, and ask two very simple questions: "How can we help?" and "Can we talk about building a world of enduring peace and prosperity?" Military intervention would be allowed only when authorized by Congress in accordance with the US Constitution. Some people around the globe would welcome us as advocates of peace and humanity; others would not allow us to teach and work with them to rebuild their civilization. But people around the globe want to restore their lives and communities, and things are different today, as we enter the twenty-first century we don't have to send out peace advocates. We can build enduring peace and prosperity without invading anyone or spending billions on a war on terrorism. We now have the means to reach people around the globe through modern technology. The Internet and cell phones allow anyone to communicate with almost anyone else. The rulers no longer have absolute control; they have to listen to the people, or *the people* will no longer tolerate or cooperate with their insidious corruption.

We will restore humanity around the globe when we retake control of our lives, stand up to corruption, and share the values on which human progress must be built. The peace advocates are going to be everywhere. They are going to restore civilization by teaching the need for personal opportunity (freedom) and personal responsibility (values like honesty and respect). The absence of core values and long-term planning dates back to the 1900s.

> The year 1919 brought swift disillusionment as the British clamped down on unrest in the Punjab, Afghanistan, and Egypt with no more than a murmur from the Americans, Wilson's star waned quickly, and Mao Zedong, Jawaharlal Nehru, and Ho Chi Minh were just some of the young nationalists activists around the world pushed left by the return of empire.
>
> Mark Mazower, *Governing the World: The History of an Idea*, 2012

It's important to understand that British and American empire building at the beginning of the twentieth century created the conditions that led to the growth and spread of oppressive governing and communism, the promise that "benevolent collectivism" would provide justice and economic stability. As we are well aware, communism was a con job. In the modern age, American empire building has created the conditions that have resulted in the growth of terrorism. All people want hope, control, and respect, and again and again they put their trust and lives in the hands of thugs and continue to make unbelievable mistakes. Now we are faced with the choice—more empire building and reliance on force, or build the moral foundation humanity requires. Are we going to descend into a new round of violence and protests? An understanding of how to promote peace and prosperity around the world didn't exist in 1919, and it still does not exist today. In *Governing the World: The History of an Idea*, Mark Mazower, a professor of history at Columbia University, documents the fact that over the past two hundred years, intellectual leadership has been totally clueless about how to govern and build civilization. While his book is about governing the world, he never addresses the question of how we can build a world of enduring peace and prosperity. Knowing what has happened in our history is very important, but equally important is understanding why those events happened and what people did wrong that led to such disasters. The underlying problem is the absence of moral leadership. What are our prospects of addressing and solving any of our growing problems like pollution, terrorism, poverty, and mediocre education if we won't be honest with ourselves and talk about the underlying cause of those problems?

Humanity has been deceived over and over by emperors who say, "Just follow me down this path and everything will be okay." But when they are asked what we must do to solve our problems and achieve enduring cooperation around the globe, their answer usually involves reliance on force. Today every problem is to be addressed with more legislation, obedience, and subservience. But reliance on institutional obedience and violence is not how civilizations prosper. A successful society must be built on the best qualities of human character, the personal convictions that are essential to solving our problems, differences, and challenges. What history should teach us—if we stand for nothing, we will fall or anything.

The twentieth century witnessed unbelievable progress in technology and our scientific knowledge of the world around us, and those advances have made daily life so much easier. But the twentieth century also was largely void of any quest for the moral convictions upon which civilization must be built.

Welcome to the future (if our children are to have one).

Lesson 4: The values and principles necessary to sustain civilization are not difficult to understand. Unfortunately, our modern "intellectuals" have us living in a delusional mental fog, and rather than building civilizations and a better future. My generations failure has be the complacency and silence about those core values and long-term planning on which humanity must be built.

5 Boom and Bust

I copied the following from an online news report.

> The off-shore tax havens of at least 30
> Americans accused of fraud, money laundering
> or other financial crimes have been unearthed
> in a groundbreaking report by The International
> Consortium of Investigative Journalists and a
> global consortium of news outlets. The first articles
> based on a cache of 2.5 million files were published
> Thursday, exposing secrets of more than 120,000
> offshore entities—including shell corporations and
> legal structures known as trusts—used to hide
> the finances of politicians, crooks and others from
> more than 170 nations. These havens are harboring
> an enormous amount of money. One study
> estimated the total could be as high as $32 trillion.
> That's roughly the size of the U.S. and Japanese
> economies combined.
>
> *Constantine von Hoffman, CBS MoneyWatch,*
> *April 2013*

The growing poverty and economic disparity in our country is no accident; it is financial collapse unfolding right before our eyes. There are three causes of this imminent collapse. We have to address these flaws in our modern culture.

1. oppressive taxes
2. wealth hidden in off-shore accounts
3. the deliberate devaluation of our currency (inflation)

The richest people in the world will not spend five minutes discussing what would be required to rebuild a humane society and addressing their complacency about growing poverty. We admire them for all their charity, but there is more they need to do. Instead of just "looking good," they need to stand up for what is right—and address what has gone wrong.

Here is how I see the current dysfunctional system. Here is why we are witness the growing gap between the haves and the have-nots.

Those in power manage the economy so that it has ups and downs, bubbles and bursts. The most recent example is happening in 2013. The economy has been in a slump since the last bubble burst, and the politicians and economists say they want to restore prosperity. Since 2008, millions of working Americans have seen their savings disappear and home values collapse. Repairing the economy means restoring people's confidence to borrow, spend, buy on credit, invest, and thereby create another economic bubble. Why do our leaders want bubbles and bursts?

The answer is not complicated: financial investors want the economy to collapse. When it does, they watch and wait until the Federal Reserve and government stimulus spending begin to reinvigorate the economy. Oh, the stimulus spending is not really money. The Fed opens accounts with billions of dollars typed in the deposit column and then spends the fake money on financial institutions that in turn spend the money to stimulate economic activity. (The Federal Reserve Bank was created in 1913 to regulate banks and give government more control over economic variables such as interest rates and money supply.)

According to the news reports I've seen online, the Federal Reserve in 2013 is pumping something like $80 billion a month into the financial markets to boost the economy. (I searched the Internet for "Fed stimulus spending," and among the results were several similarly worded reports that "the U.S. central bank appeared unfazed by concerns that its $85 billion in monthly bond purchases could disrupt financial markets or inflate asset bubbles.")

This means we are facing another financial bubble.

But it gets worse. The Fed also has kept interest rates near zero to encourage borrowing and add even more "stimulus money" into the economy. When investors are convinced that the economy is making a recovery, they start buying stocks, betting the stock market will reach new highs—as it is has been doing in 2013. These investors buy stocks, watching very carefully what the Fed, the US government, other financial institutions, and consumers are doing. When they see evidence of the next collapse, when the next bubble is ready to burst, they sell their stocks and make millions (and the bubble collapses). Then they invest (hide) their new wealth in banks offshore, where they have to pay little in taxes. In the meantime, working folks suddenly find their savings have disappeared.

When government feeds money into the economy, "stimulus spending", it causes inflation. When investors remove money from the economy, it diminishes the amount of capital available for business investment. And when both happen at the same time, it results in what economists call "stagflation." Then the rich wait for the economy to recover and they start the process all over again. These investors pocket millions and billions in profits while doing nothing constructive. It's called playing the system. Over the decades, the rich have gotten rich doing nothing but sitting by the pool and drinking martinis, while the middle class is slowly being destroyed. Too bad. That's why the rich want to create booms and busts and why the middle class is being wiped out of existence. That is why there is such growing disparity and distrust between working people and the elites. I call it "pragmatic capitalism"—meaning there are no positive values or long-term planning guiding investors, consumers, or public policies.

As an alternative, we should insist that the Fed publish a statement on how it would protect our currency and the economy from such manipulations. That statement should include a description of a *free market with moral values*. If those who run the Fed cannot define such monetary policies, they should all be fired. I would give them a severance package: two weeks pay at a rate equivalent to what an employee at McDonald's or Walmart makes. Monetary policy would then be returned to the government, which has promised to answer to the people. The government would then publish for public review the monetary and economic policies which would protect the nation's currency and middle class. Protecting citizens from manipulation of the currency is what legitimate government is supposed to do. Such explicit guidelines would give both investors and consumers confidence that long-range financial security is something they can count on.

> From its creation in 1913, the most important Fed mandate has been to maintain the purchasing power of the dollar; however, since 1913 the dollar has lost over 95 percent of its value. Put differently, it takes twenty dollars today to buy what one dollar would buy in 1913.
>
> James Rickards, *Currency Wars: The Making of the Next Global Crisis*, 2012

Since the 1930s, the government, in cahoots with the Federal Reserve, has reduced the purchasing power of our currency by well over 2,000 percent. It would now take twenty dollars to buy what one dollar would buy back in 1913. A minimum wage or paycheck today with the same purchasing power would have to be over fifteen dollars an hour. Inflation makes life-sustaining products and services ever more expensive, and so more and more people end up living paycheck to paycheck—if they have a job at all. Too bad for all those working citizens and parents who wanted to build a better future for their children. The primary reason families cannot afford health care, a college education, or food on their table is the devaluation of the currency—inflation. The first time I bought a first-class postage stamp it cost four cents; now a stamp costs forty-six cents. That's more than a 1,000 percent increase. I have read some of the books by our nation's "financial experts," and I can't determine whether they are deliberately perpetrating a fraud or are just incompetent. What's clear, however, is that the American people have been duped into living in a financial scam that is ultimately going to collapse.

Money doesn't grow on trees. Wealth is the product of creative, productive, responsible, honest effort. People cannot spend more than they produce. A nation cannot prosper on deficit spending. There is no free ride. Those who promise economic security with more government regulations and spending are taking us down the yellow brick road. Money (currency) used in the production and exchange of goods and services *must* represent a reliable, consistent exchange rate—a fixed, known, every lasting value.

> We make money the old-fashioned way. We print it.
> Art Rolnick, former chief economist, Minneapolis Federal Reserve Bank

Over the next ten years we must phase out all stimulus spending, welfare programs, subsidies, benefits, and bailouts made at taxpayers' expense. We must care for the homeless and forgotten through voluntary assistance programs, because if we continue down the current path we are going to witness growing disparity, poverty, and financial chaos. When this cataclysm erupts, our trusted government will take control of our savings and checking accounts and we will be living in a police state. To save us from the looming disaster, we must cut government spending by something like 70 percent. We also must cut military spending by 50 percent and shut down the CIA altogether. (For more read, *Legacy of Ashes* by Tim Weiner) The only way to restore and maintain economic prosperity is for citizens to take control of their own finances and government provides a stable currency. If we keep using excuses to evade this personal responsibility, financial security of families, and the economy are headed for bankrupt. By phasing out welfare, government bailouts, subsidies, and deficit spending, we can cut the tax rate to less than 15 percent of earnings for every working American. Then we all could afford the kind of education, health care, retirement, and financial security that we should be able to expect. Such changes will not be easy, but in a relatively short amount of time we will have achieved something that does not exist today—long-range economic security.

> Between 1990 and 2000 the compensation awarded to the head of Citigroup rose 12,444 percent while that of the average schoolteacher in New York went up 20 percent. Meanwhile, 15 percent of the population lives below the (officially defined) poverty level, 5.5 million are in the criminal justice system, and as of 2002, more than 2 million are in prison—the highest per capita rate of incarceration in the world, 1 per 143.
> Morris Berman, *Dark Ages America: The Final Phase of Empire*, 2006

There is an alternative to the current unsustainable corrupt system. Starting now we need to set forth a new form of economy—I call it the People Investment Economy, or PIE. It's an economic system in which corporations are not viewed as people, and all people are treated with respect, not reduced to living like pathetic slaves of governments. Under this shared moral values and expectations, we would take back control of our lives and finances—something we must do if we are going to behave like responsible adults.

Under the PIE system, we do business only with locally owned banks and credit unions. We buy products made locally. We do not buy high-tech cell phones, fancy shoes, or baseball caps made in China or America with slave labor. We do not buy corporate-manufactured food laced with chemicals and pesticides. We do not thrive on FDA-approved drugs. We do not drive around in gas-guzzling autos. We do not do business with or shop at stores where the CEOs make millions while paying their employees ten dollars an hour. We do not put our savings and retirement accounts in the stock market; we invest in local businesses so we know how our money is being used and managed. We do not watch disgusting entertainment obsessed with violence and nonsense. We do not attend sporting events with players who are paid millions; we participate in local sports activities. We do not eat junk food, confident that taxpayers will pay for our health care. We act like people instead of mindless consumers. We take control and responsibility for our lives and finances because what is what we have to do. I eat red meat only once a month and spend half my food budget on fresh fruits and vegetables. (To take control of your health, read *The RAVE Diet & Lifestyle* by Mike Anderson.)

The next time you're sitting in a classroom, lecture hall, or church, look around you. Do these friends and neighbors have strong moral values? Do they talk about long range prospects, or are they relying on fancy excuses to justify living as parasites on the backs of taxpayers and future generations? We have the daily responsibility to judge how we manage public policies as a nation and manage our lives as individuals. Ultimately, the conditions we live with and endure are a product of our own expectations and convictions.

> Because we no longer have a moral compass to guide our political system, we now face the possibility of economic and social upheaval. Without a moral foundation to our political system it's a free-for-all, and those who understand how to use government power benefit the most.
>
> Ron Paul, *Liberty Defined: 50 Essential Issues that Affect Our Freedom, 2011*

What are our children to think if we will not talk honestly about those personal choices and public policies? Are we supposed to remain silent because these kinds of issues are not our responsibility? Apparently that is what our educators, commentators, and news reporters would have us believe, because we're living in a world of spin. Today, those leading us into collapse bear no accountability, and if we wish to hold them accountable, we first must hold ourselves accountable. We must recognize that there is no free ride, although the emperors what us to believe them as they keep making promises to keep us all living like lost sheep and mindless consumers.

Lesson 5: The rich insist on reliance on government, manipulate the military-corporate-welfare-state complex, to manage citizen's most personal choices and finances. Those in power are not held accountable and will do almost anything to protect their secret path to control and plunder. We now live in a form of communism that we are told is democracy. The measure of personal success must be pursued through self-realization, building and advancing humanity, instead of hiding million and billions in off shore banks.

6 *Living like Subjects*

Here is what happens in a society that relies on brute force to solve problems. Here is how rulers conduct public policy when they refuse to respect citizens. Here is what happens when we allow ourselves to be treated like doormats.

When I was in college, our government was drafting young people and sending them into war. I avoided the draft, but it became clear to me that the Vietnam War was just more evidence that our leaders were tyrants with little regard for America's youth. At my school, Ohio State University, student protests against the war were ongoing, and protesters had occupied the administration building. I walked out of my way to avoid any of the campus protests.

At Kent State, things got out of hand, as described in this account from Wikipedia.

When it was determined the crowd was not going to disperse, a group of 77 National Guard troops from A Company and Troop G, with bayonets fixed on their M1 Garand rifles, began to advance upon the hundreds of protesters. As the guardsmen advanced, the protesters retreated up and over Blanket Hill, heading out of The Commons area.

At 12:24 pm, according to eyewitnesses, a Sgt. Myron Pryor turned and began firing at the students with his .45 pistol. A number of guardsmen nearest the students also turned and fired their M1 Garand rifles at the students. In all, 29 of the 77 guardsmen claimed to have fired their weapons, using a final total of 67 rounds of ammunition.

The shootings killed four students and wounded nine. Two of the four students killed, Allison Krause and Jeffrey Miller, had participated in the protest, and the other two, Sandra Scheuer and William Knox Schroeder, had been walking from one class to the next at the time of their deaths. Schroeder was also a member of the campus <u>ROTC</u> battalion. Of those wounded, none was closer than 71 feet to the guardsmen. Of those killed, the nearest (Miller) was 265 feet away, and their average distance from the guardsmen was 345 feet.

The questions any such tragedy should raise are: What went wrong? What must we do differently to prevent such an atrocity from happening again? What should we learn from this incident? After all, it wasn't just an accident; it was deliberate.

Here is the truth that our incompetent leaders and educators do not want discussed: if the voters, the National Guard, and college students had received an education on basic moral values, this massacre never would have happened.

Whether by their own initiative or by order of their commanders, some of America's finest aimed their military weapons at American college students and pulled the trigger, again and again and again.

If basic moral principles had been taught, these National Guard soldiers, whether acting on their own or on orders from commanders, would have said, "No, I will not murder innocent people." And the guard unit commanders, upon receiving orders to dispatch military forces to a college campus, would have said to their commanders, "Are you crazy?" And the politicians who supported another unjustified war would have been voted out of office for making such a waste of the US military, America's youth, and of human lives. And those college students would not have been protesting because this unjustified war would never have been allowed to go on year after year. But most important, we should have recognized that those students (like me) never would have found themselves sitting in college classrooms where the teachers or professors refused to recognize or teach the importance of and need for moral principles.

Nothing has changed in the forty years since the Kent State shooting. In fact, the underlying problem has only gotten worse. Here in Denver we have witnessed the Columbine school massacre (1999) and, a few miles from my home, the Aurora theater massacre (2012). We now have out breaks of violence across the nation almost on a monthly basis. Such random killings are acts of hopelessness and revenge against a society that does not respect its citizens. Politicians and commentators love to talk and talk about these events, but other than a discussion of the alleged need for more laws, security measures, and psychiatric care, there has not been one word about addressing the root causes of such violence. As with the War on Drugs, the War on Poverty, and the War on Terrorism, we are led to believe that the War on Violence requires more government, more police, more security in our schools, and three strikes and you out crime prevention. There is no recognized need to address the real, underlying problem.

When someone is in a position of power—whether he is a member of the CIA, the FBI, the local police, the National Guard, or the US military—and ordered to initiate the use of deadly force against American's best (college students who are doing nothing but protecting their government) he must exercise moral judgment. It is everyone's moral responsibility to say, No, when asked or ordered to commit an atrocity. The torture and killing of innocent people is something we all have to stand up to and reject unequivocally. We should be proud of our police and our military because they protect our liberties, but when the emperors up on stage are turning us into a police state or a global empire, it is the moral obligation of those who are expected to carry out the oppression to stand up and say, No. Refusal to blindly obey or carry out policies of oppression is an act of patriotism. The future of America depends more on what we the people do than our military.

It is everyone's responsibility to know, revere, and support the inalienable rights of everyone to life, liberty, and the pursuit of happiness. It is citizen's responsibility in a free society to insist upon governing that protects, and not enslave or intimidate, its citizens.

Our collective silence makes us part of the problem. If we do not stand up for our shared ideals, those corrupt emperors and their special interests will secretly use government to force us into perpetual servitude.

I describe the society we now inhabit as a nation running on empty. What I mean is that we endure constant debate about political issues but complete silence about the relevant moral arguments. Commentators love and get paid to talk about what's happening in Washington and around the globe, but they refuse to talk about how to put us back on a path to civilization, which is necessary if we are to achieve enduring peace and prosperity. Honesty in media means providing the essential information to address and solve a problem. When our news outlets refuse to provide this essential information, they are lying to us, virtually every day. So, for a change, let's make the moral argument about an ongoing human crisis, and end the growing oppression and needless wars. We cannot promote peace around the globe with force and military threats; it requires an explicit vision that inspires people to cooperate and work together.

A decade ago, American news commentators should have been informing everyone about the corruption manifest in Middle Eastern countries like Egypt, Syria, Iran, Iraq, Turkey, and Israel. For example, when our government was funding the military dictator in Egypt with more than a billion of our hard-earned tax dollars every year, we should have been informed about the corruption in Egypt and all these other countries. We then could have been informing the citizens and leaders of those nations how to build healthy communities. When peaceful protests broke out in the Middle East, we could have provided valid principles and a vision that would form a foundation for a fair society—a society that offers the kind of opportunity that people want and expect in life and from their government. When any citizens or rulers resorted to violence or using weapons of any kind, we could have recognized them for what they were—morally deprived— and taken steps to make them face their crimes against innocent people. We might have imposed sanctions that punished the leaders while giving hope to the oppressed.

However, history tells us that sanctions, the use of force against sovereign countries, has consequences. Sanctions imposed on Iraq by the United Nations, United States, and England from 1990 to 2003 resulted in the deaths of more than one hundred thousand children. (To learn more, Google "Iraqi sanctions.") Whether those children died from the use of chemical weapons or from starvation from imposed sanctions, their murder was an act of moral depravity. Had we been informed of those deaths at the time, we would not have supported or tolerated any such crimes.

What should we recommend as a solution? We should encourage the victims of the inhumanities to stand up for their rights.

The hundreds of thousands of families displaced as result of the ongoing civil war in Syria, refugees living in temporary camps, should make signs stating, "We come in peace. We will never use weapons, violence, or force against anyone." Then, carrying those signs, they should move back home to restart their lives, rebuild their communities, and work for a government that respects and protects everyone's rights and liberties. That is the moral path—and it represents a vision that today's politicians, commentators, and emperors do not want to talk about because it recognizes the inherent competence and potential of all citizens to solve their societies' problems. Then, if any group or nation—the rebels, the United States, Russia, Syria, or Iran—initiated or enabled the slaughter of innocent people, families rebuilding their lives, they would be recognized for what they were—morally deprived. Instead of threatening to launch missiles into Syria, we should have been sending messages to both the military and the rebels to stop committing crimes against humanity. Then, hopefully, people would stop supporting, funding, and cooperating with such corruption.

The future of mankind rests with people who exercise personal conviction working in harmony with their neighbors. The pending collapse is the consequence of people who believe they are better off living as subject of their government. Again, we now live in a world where the only solution to societal problems is the use of force and intimidation. What we endure today is deliberate, ongoing blindness about how to build a better future. What we need is a new path, the moral path.

We come in peace, we will never use weapons, violence, or force against anyone. What moral convictions does such a message convey? It conveys a willingness to be *honest* and *respect* the rights of everyone, because that is what being human, in the best sense, requires.

Yes, most adults will agree that values are important. But try to find one adult who understands that being a person of character means taking responsibility for everything one says and does. Honesty requires defining those personal convictions explicitly, so they are something more than vague generalities. The evidence of our government's ongoing dishonesty, elaborate excuses, and corruption is right in front of us and has been getting worse for decades.

> Listening to bureaucrats and politicians boast about the drug war, you have to wonder what they are smoking. The war on drugs has been one of the biggest public policy disasters of the last twenty-five years. It has not reduced drug use; it has instead increased violent crime attendant on illegal drug trafficking, and police corruption, just as the prohibition of alcohol increased criminal activity and graft in the 1920s. It has eroded civil liberties, particularly constitutional protection against unwarranted searches and seizures.
>
> Wendy Kaminer, *Sleeping with Extra-Terrestrials: The Rise of Irrationalism and Perils of Piety, 1999*

The reason we've endured decades of drug and alcohol abuse, crime, violence, suicide, and financial collapse is because we have been suckered into believing that laws, bureaucrats, prisons, and "three strikes and you're out" nonsense would solve these kinds of problems. To solve the problem of persistent, destructive behavior, we have to define a set of moral values that enable everyone in our society to exercise basic self-realization and make the most of his or her opportunities in life.

The debate over illegal immigration in America would be an example. Back in 2012, the president visited South America, where he was asked to discuss the drug wars killing hundreds of Central and South American citizens. Our neighbors know who buys the drugs and sells the guns to the drug smugglers, and they wanted to talk about the problem. Our president's response to the concerned leaders of Central and South America—silence.

Solving the immigration problem, we are told, will require $47 billion for the militarization of the Mexican border. I look forward to the day when someone stands next to the border and says (as President Reagan did about the Berlin Wall), "Take down this fence." When governments build walls and fences, it is because the only "solution" they know involves more threats, intimidation, and military spending. Instead of solving the problem, they are wasting taxpayers' money and perpetuating the growing violence and drug wars. They like drug wars because they fund our burgeoning corporate prison system. It represents the current assumption, the spin and propaganda, that government is the solution to all our problems.

How can we solve the problems of drug and alcohol abuse and crime that now plague our nation? We must begin by understanding their cause. The reason so many people resort to self-destructive lifestyles is that they have no expectations of making something of their lives. The American Dream no longer exists for those who feel left out. In order to restore people's confidence in themselves, we must restore both the opportunity of a fulfilling life and the convictions upon which personal ambition and confidence must be built. We must start treating people like people rather than subjects, morons, and slaves.

Our government leaders want to keep us under their thumb. If they recognized that we are competent citizens, they would have to talk about and do away with the oppressive government that now has us living like slaves. That is the change, the new path they do not want anyone talking about. They maintain power and control by perpetuating the notion that we are better off depending on rules, ideologies, and edicts. If we fail to get out from under the thumb of oppressive government, we will have no future.

Self-destructive behaviors are the consequence of character flaws. Character flaws are any kind of attitude, belief, justification, habit, or ideology that impedes and diminishes our human potential to be the best we can be.

Success in life is a product of competence and a dedication to solving problems. The ability to solve problems is what separates humans from animals, and making excuses is what renders us a burden and a hazard to those with whom we live and work. People of character have the courage and convictions to demand the best from themselves and everyone around them.

By relying on flawed ideologies, we have become used to never knowing for sure what the truth is. As a result, we cannot work together to solve problems. We cannot talk to one another because each of us lives in his or her own liberal or conservative, oppressed or elite, six-pack-guzzling, make-believe world—a self-induced fog. It isn't so much that we view the world from our own perspectives, but that our world-view is not understood or shared by anyone with a different background or beliefs from ours. We rarely experience the understanding and confidence made possible by honest communication.

Social Security is one example of groupthink—it's America's sacred cow, a social mandate that no one dare question. Because our "free society" has embraced massive welfare programs and the exploitation of working citizens, there can be no honest communication about the contradiction between individual rights and collective obedience. You have to be wearing blinders to claim you're an admirer of personal liberty while at the same time condoning programs that enslave everyone. Such a widely accepted contradiction means all debate and discussion has to be slanted to justify popular opinion. At that point public discourse on the subject comes to resemble propaganda, through which we deceive ourselves about our righteousness. Therefore America's schools cannot teach the principles on which a free society rests; in order to do so, they would have to teach that such legislated obedience represents what is "good" for people rather than a violation of our sacred principles. Rather than being honest about the propaganda machine, our educational professionals remain silent on the issue. Or worse, they facilitate the indoctrination by teaching the need for mandatory sacrifice to promote the common good. We are taught to believe that personal liberty does not work, that there are no valid principle of human conduct, and no agreement is possible.

Groupthink means: once a person or a community accepts a contradiction, every argument must conform to that contradiction; to argue otherwise means one is not supportive of our national policies, of the group mentality. Public discourse becomes a process of twisting the truth (spin) to defend the system that we should recognize as fundamentally flawed.

A country that ignores or remains silent about the principles on which it was founded cannot teach those principles. A country that practices contradictions cannot teach the virtues of honesty, integrity, and reason. A country that enslaves its citizens cannot teach respect for individual rights or demonstrate how such principles would solve the problems that now surround us. A country that does not revere its founding principles will ultimately realize it is going down a path it never should have taken. A country that tolerates formal education on every subject except personal values is a society abandoning its respect for the individual. Groupthink is habitual, systematic excuse-making that keeps us all helpless and obedient.

Lesson 6: Until we teach our children how to develop and exercise honesty, reason, and integrity and live with respect for everyone, we are headed toward societal collapse. Until we define those core values and engage in long-term planning, relying on fancy excuses, we are headed down the yellow brick road. The ongoing corruption in our society is not just happening in back alleys; it is happening in our schools, on our college campuses, and in every home in America.

7 IRS Fraud

> Thus, the State is a coercive criminal organization that subsists by a regularized large-scale system of taxation-theft, and which gets away with it by engineering the support of the majority . . . through securing an alliance with a group of opinion-molding intellectuals whom it rewards with a share in its power and pelf.
>
> Murray N. Rothbard, *The Ethics of Liberty,* 1985

I have no problem with government providing public services (with the approval of its citizens), but it has to do so honestly. When we pay gasoline taxes used exclusively for building and maintaining roads, those fees are a legitimate payment for services rendered. When government takes out thirty-year loans to build roads and bridges, it forces our children and grandchildren to pay for our highways, which is a form of corruption. Why should future generations pay for our roads? Future generations are going to have pay to maintain those roads when they grow up. Having our children pay for our highways is a strategy typical of a generation that will take whatever it can get away with.

The concept of democracy must not be misconstrued to mean anything voters or corporations can get away with, a free ride, the bailout of businesses and banks. In an honest economy, wealth is created through hard work and innovation—not through fraud, counterfeiting, taxes, or government spending.

Who is responsible for the growing numbers of homeless families—businesses that aim to make a profit honestly by providing needed goods and services, or corrupt government that confiscates half of people's earnings? The biggest drain on people's earnings is government. The biggest drag on people's standard of living is inflation. Respect for citizens starts in the home and extends all the way to the federal government.

Do we have the right to send the police into our neighbors' homes if we don't approve of how they are managing their lives?

In her book *Godless: The Church of Liberalism*, Ann Coulter asks, "But if we cannot legislate what goes on in the bedroom, why can't I hide money from the IRS under my mattress?" Guess what: as long as government is stealing people's hard-earned income, you should be hiding money from the IRS. Isn't that what the rich do routinely, with crafty loopholes, corporate subsidies, and deposits in foreign banks? If Mitt Romney can hide his wealth in off-shore banks, why can't working Americans hide their money under their mattresses?

We know why: the rule of law is slanted to protect the rich and to pick the pockets of working Americans. We are not paying for services rendered. We're playing a game rigged by the well connected and the politicians who insist they are serving the common good. The reason people feel so threatened by their government is that government has become a form of organized crime. If we care about the poor and forgotten, we have to restore their opportunity to make the most of their lives.

The rule of law means a legal system limited to protecting citizens from force, fraud, and negligence, and not a set of laws used to rob, steal, and plunder. Have you ever heard the courts or commentators address questions like whether a deliberately vague tax code is constitutional; whether there is a law that requires working Americans to pay or file federal income taxes; whether the government has the right to legislate massive, socialist programs; or whether the federal government has the authority to fund and manage education clear down to the grade-school level? The reason the courts, politicians, and professors will not address such questions is because they are afraid of upsetting the status quo, the groupthink mentality. Lawyers really don't know what principles to uphold or what *the rule of law* really means.

The income tax is unlawful because it is based on a law that is thousands of pages long, deliberately vague, arbitrary, and incomprehensible making it impossible or very expensive to comply with this law. And our legal professionals don't give a hoot, in fact, citizens and businesses pay them to comply with the tax laws. To bypass these violations of citizens' rights, the IRS does not prosecute tax violators. Instead it confiscates people's hard-earned money without ever filing charges, taking them before a jury, or giving them an opportunity to defend themselves in a court of law. It is corrupt, and the "legal profession" stands by and does nothing. The IRS is nothing less than a form of organized crime. (See *IRS Humbug: IRS Weapons of Enslavement* by Frank Kowalik.)

Under our Constitution, any tax whose intended purpose is to *redistribute wealth* is a violation of individual rights. This raises the question, what about progressive taxes, which are lower for the poor and higher for the rich? There is nothing immoral about a progressive tax system, because the wealthy who own and manage businesses add the cost of their taxes necessary to operating their business to the price of their products and services. Thus the poor who spend most of their earnings on those goods and services are paying the taxes businesses have included in the cost of doing business. Thus, a fair income tax might be 15 percent of all income over $30,000 per year. Anyone earning less than $30,000 a year would pay no income taxes. The poor are paying their fair share every time they buy goods and services.

Lesson 7: If we continue to cooperate with, vote for, and pay the taxes that fund the government that is destroying our future, who is to blame? Responsible politicians would restore constitutional government. Then citizens would have good reason to pay their taxes because government would be performing it's legitimate function—the protection of everyone from corrupt governing, criminal behavior, and fraudulent business scams.

Legitimate government provides the foundation for building the castle on the hill, the public forum where citizens discuss, share, and implement the core values and long-term expectations to build a better future for their children.

8 The Rule of Law

The following quotations represent two very different views of the rule of law. The question we citizens must answer is this: What kind of government should we demand—one that respects and protects our rights, or one that routinely treats people like doormats? We can live in a society that encourages people to make the most of their opportunities in life, or we can endure one that relies on coercion to confiscate and redistribute citizens' earnings. If we cannot reach some agreement on that question, what are our prospects for solving societal problems?

> Our legislators are not sufficiently appraised of the rightful limits of their power; that their true office is to declare and enforce our natural rights and duties, and to take none of them from us. No man has a natural right to commit aggression on the equal rights of another; and this is all from which the laws ought to restrain him; every man is under the natural duty of contributing to the necessities of the society; and this is all the laws should enforce on him; and, no man having the right to be the judge between himself and another, it is his natural duty to submit to the umpirage of an impartial third party. When the laws have declared and enforced all

this, they have fulfilled their functions; and the idea is quite unfounded, that on entering into society we give up any natural right.

Thomas Jefferson

A Constitution is not intended to embody a particular economic theory, whether of paternalism and the organic relation of the citizen to the state or of laissez fair. It is made for people of fundamentally differing views, and of accident of our finding certain opinions natural and familiar, or novel, and even shocking, ought not to conclude our judgment upon the question whether statutes embodying them conflict with the Constitution of the United States.

Justice Oliver Wendell Holmes Jr., 1841-1935

Thomas Jefferson is recognizing the principle that the law, the government and the courts serve to protect the rights of citizens. Justice Oliver Wendell Holmes, in contrast, is promoting the idea that that there are no principles upon which the laws of the nation should be built. He sounds just like our modern philosophers. Some ten-year-old should have told the justice about the closely guarded secret not talked about in the halls of government—that America stands for the rights of everyone to live free of servitude. Under Justice Holmes's interpretation, government becomes whatever people want it to be so they can escape personal responsibility, and government representatives and the Supreme Court can interpret the law any way they choose. Anything goes if special interests, lobbyists, or the majority can get away with it or find an attorney who understands how use the vagueness of the rules to their advantage.

> Indeed, the United States now has the exact opposite of a single set of laws before which everyone is equal. It has an entrenched two-tiered system of justice: the country's most powerful political and financial elites are virtually immunized from the rule of law, empowered to commit felonies with full-scale impunity and to act without any constraints, while the politically powerless are imprisoned with greater ease and in far greater numbers than any country on the planet.
>
> Glenn Greenwald, *With Liberty and Justice for Some,* 2011

What we should conclude, if we are ever seated on a jury, is that regardless of what instructions the judge hands down, we citizens have the right and responsibility to refuse to convict anyone for violations of unconstitutional laws. Here in Colorado, the federal government does not enforce its laws prohibiting the manufacture, use, or possession of marijuana because when the accused is taken before a jury, he or she is almost always found innocent. That's called jury nullification. The right to a trial by jury and the right to jury nullification are part of every citizen's constitutional rights.

Put very simply, in a free society people are expected to provide for their families and care for one another voluntarily. When government promises to protect the lowest on the ladder, virtually everyone learns to live as victims, dependents, and beneficiaries of the system—especially the well-off who have become expert at playing the system. We now see the long-term result: over half of people's earning is confiscated by government; and nearly half the nation's population lives on government benefits, subsidies, and handouts. Congratulations! We have become a nation of freeloaders living on the backs of our children. Through force and intimidation, the most powerful are going to control the wealth while the rest of us are the suckers, the peons, and (of course) the "problem" that requires further government assistance.

> *United States v. O'Brien*, 1968: Sustained the conviction of a young man who violated a federal law by burning his draft card, explaining that he did so in order to influence others to adopt his antiwar beliefs. The Court said that an incidental limitation on First Amendment freedom is justified if (a) it is within the constitutional power of the government; (b) it furthers an important substantial government interest; (c) the government interest is unrelated to the suppression of free expression; and (d) the incidental restriction on alleged First Amendment freedoms is no greater than is essential to the furtherance of that interest.
>
> Edward Conrad Smith, *The Constitution of the United States with Case Summaries, 1979*

The principles set forth in *United States v. O'Brien* suggest that if some of our young people protested the welfare state and burned their Social Security cards with the intent of influencing others to adopt their anti-socialist beliefs, they would be arrested, convicted, and thrown in jail. Exercising their right to free expression and standing up for their rights means they would be prosecuted under our current legal system.

What does it mean when the restriction of our liberties is acceptable if the government's interest is unrelated to the suppression, as claimed in *United States v. O'Brien*? Are there such things as First Amendment freedoms according to this ruling, or are such rights just allegations by uninformed protestors? This ruling means that being opposed to corrupt government programs and policies, and protesting such programs and policies, could get you arrested and thrown in jail. Does that sound like a free society or a police state? Clearly the government that was established to protect us is now an institution of insidious harassment and enslavement.

If the country descends into a police state, the members of the Supreme Court and the legal profession will declare it's not their fault—but it will be their fault. When the government passes laws that serve to dictate people's lives and the court declares them constitutional, the court is spinning the web we are all trapped in. The rule of law has become the rule of the lawless.

On a June 9, 2013, episode of *60 Minutes*, Scott Pelley interviewed US Supreme Court Justice Sonia Sotomayor. The subjects of the role of the courts in America, the principles guiding the courts, recent court rulings, the vital role of the Supreme Court, the vital need for understanding the role of the courts, or the growing intrusion of government into people's private lives *never* came up in the interview. What should that fact tell us about our news media? It's another example of talk with no substance and the ongoing silence about the most important challenges facing this nation.

Lesson 8: What we do in the next five years will define what kind of people we are and what kind of nation we are. The keys to turning the lights back on are not complicated. We must . . .

- ☐ fix the tax code (get it down to less than five pages) to get the government off the backs of our children;
- ☐ restore the rule of law so that it is absolutely clear about what is requires of citizens and serves to protects citizens rights and liberties;
- ☐ teach the essential values upon which our future success depends; which will require talking to our children honestly.

9 Becoming a New Person

Imagine a group of fourth graders listening to a lecture on personal values and accountability (something I never heard in any class). At the conclusion of the lecture, the teacher asks if there are any questions. Johnny puts up his hand and asks, "Does this mean I am free to leave and don't have to return if I see no benefit to what is being taught?"

The response: "Yes, Johnny. That is what we expect of you. That is what being responsible means."

Now imagine an ethics class in our current education system, in which the teacher keeps secret the fact that he admires Social Security, government-run education, and massive military spending; drives a gas-guzzling SUV to a home in the suburbs; shops at a grocery store to buy chemical-laced food with little nutritional value; has a big, energy-inefficient home with no vegetable garden; and enjoys entertainment that is mostly degrading. How would such a teacher provide moral guidance or serve as a role model?

We can take this example one step further. When America actually starts to provide ethics instruction, the students are going to want to know *everything* about their teachers, and the teachers are going to want to know *everything* about their students—where they live, what they like best about life, what values they revere, and what goals and aspirations they have in life. Why? Because knowing and caring about our neighbors is the foundation of a civil society. Civil society means knowing what shared ideas and values hold the community together. The source of the best of humanity, of basic respect and appreciation for our fellow citizens, is the shared expectation of building better lives for everyone. That is why the teaching of ethics is vital to our success and happiness. When you see schools plagued by bullying and federally mandated testing (and armed guards walking the corridors), the underlying problem is the absence of any shared moral principles.

Throughout the course of every day, we spend a fair amount of time in buildings, man-made structures that provide a place to work, live, and study. Notice that while we're in one of these structures we all have a substantial degree of confidence that the floor under our feet or the roof over our heads is not going to collapse. We feel safe in those buildings because the people who designed and built them did so with knowledge, integrity, personal expectations and convictions to do their best. We feel safe because of the skills, knowledge, and dedication reflected in a *job well done* and *best behavior*. Now, with that example in mind, ask yourself this: Can we be confidant the air we breathe, the water we drink, and the food we eat is safe if we don't teach, revere, and practice shared convictions?

Quality education would build enduring confidence and trust in ourselves and one another. What would character building look like if we were to provide such education?

Character development would start at home, in community organizations, and in elementary schools (and on-line education). Students would spend time addressing questions about human choices, discussing and evaluating how they would respond to the challenges they were going to be faced with out in the real world. The purpose of such a discussion would be to identify, test, validate, and examine in detail the qualities that lead to enduring success and self-confidence, and how to distinguish those qualities from contrived excuses. Students would be encouraged to bring up any question or concern that they wanted addressed. At the end of the discussion, students would be able to identify dishonesty, spin, and deliberate fraud within a minute or less. They would know who was deceiving them and whom they should work with and trust. Most important, they would know what kind of person they should strive to be. Teachers would be role models instead of disciplinarians. In a fairly short time, public trust and confidence in our community and our nation would inspire citizens rather than demeaning them. A sense of personal responsibility would replace indifference and apprehension. And we could be confident that every product and service brought to the market was based on a foundation of personal integrity.

History will record who led America into collapse. Politicians will be blamed and deserve that blame, but the real culprits are all graduates of Harvard, Yale, Princeton, and other modern universities that are the source of today's delusional thinking. That's why after reading this book you'll be smarter than the average college professor. You'll know what is destroying your future, and you can spread the word about what has to change. Great change starts around the dining room table. Change is the result of knowledge, determination, and courage.

Here is more evidence of that delusional thinking:

Without a definition and identifiable grounds for morality, belief in the relativism of values and nihilism were encouraged. Morality was simply relative to each society and each person. It was either an expression of personal chosen moral beliefs or merely an unpredictable and individual expression of emotions. In either case, no basis exists for people to reach common moral understanding.

Norma Haan, Eliane Aerts, and Bruce A. G. Cooper, *On Moral Grounds: The Search for Practical Morality, 1985*

Many philosophers would say that they cannot establish correct theories about how one ought to live, because no one can do so. There is, they would say, no such thing as a "correct" view about how one ought to live, since beliefs about such matters cannot properly be said to be either true or false. Rather, they should be understood as expressions of feelings or attitudes, choices or commitments, and if people differ from one another in their basic attitudes about what is good or right, there is in principle no way of resolving the disagreement, no "correct" answer to be arrived at.

Richard Norman, *The Moral Philosophers: An Introduction to Ethics, 1983*

Want to know why we are headed down the path to collapse? Because we are lead to believe that "no basis exists for people to reach common moral understanding." And, "there is in principle no way of resolving the disagreement, no 'correct' answer to be arrived at." This brings us back to where we started. The problem is that our intellectual leaders have no respect for or confidence in people.

Nothing is going to change until we start to teach a set of values and ideals upon which a successful civilization must be built. Educators at all levels should teach, examine, and build on those essential qualities of character. Once they do, we will soon be living in whole new world.

Instead of accepting defeat, regimentation, and abuse, young people should refuse to be treated like doormats. Teenagers should refuse to register for a Social Security number, refuse to sit in a classroom where the teacher won't articulate or build on valid principles. Adults should take a good look at themselves in the mirror and ask themselves what they can do differently, because the benevolent government is going bankrupt. This time America needs to decide what liberty really means, instead of engaging in yet more talk with no substance.

Here's one example of how young people can change the world. Here is an example of how children are often well aware of how slow and silent adults are to doing what must be done.

Nine months before Rosa Parks refused to give up her seat on a bus in the segregated South, (1955) setting off the civil rights movement, a fifteen-year-old girl did the very same thing—refused to give up her seat on a bus in the segregated South. She was arrested and hauled off by the police.

There are two things you should do. First, get this book into the hands of your friends. Second, start talking about what has gone wrong and what we must do to save America. In a very short time, people will be going back to work and bureaucrats will be out of a job. People will be talking to one another instead of laying blame, pointing fingers, and making excuses. And, the emperors dressed in fancy clothes, feeding the propaganda machine, will get laughed off stage. Politicians instead of making false promises would be doing their jobs, fulfilling their role and purpose in a free society.

On September 11, 2001, the day of the bombing of the World Trade Center, America made a huge mistake. We had the attention of the world. We had the sympathy of the world. We had the opportunity to lead other nations in addressing the growing hatred and violence around the world. And we did exactly the wrong thing. Instead of joining in a mission to build a better world, working with everyone, we proclaimed a War on Terror. We began relying on force, torture, secret prisons, and surveillance of citizens. We again proved we don't trust our own citizens, that we don't hold any values, that we're willing to live by or define a model for other nations. We have abandoned our conviction to do what must be done, and instead we've made more enemies. We have played right into the hands of those who want to destroy us. As Abraham Lincoln warned, we are destroying our self.

A constitution is a document that defines the principles citizens intend to live by. It is supposed to be the rock solid foundation on which the castle on the hill is built. What follows are portions of Iraq's constitution, voted in on October 15, 2005. Every word of it was reviewed and approved by the (incompetent) leaders of the U. S. government.

Article 30:
First: The state guarantee to the individual and the family—especially children and women—social

and health security and the basic requirements for leading a free and dignified life. The state also ensures the above suitable income and appropriate housing.

Second: The state guarantees the social and health security to Iraqis in cases of old age, sickness, employment disability, homelessness, orphanage or unemployment, and shall work to protect them from ignorance, fear, and poverty. The State shall provide them housing and special programs of care and rehabilitation. This will be organized by law.

Article 31:

First: Every citizen has the right to health care. The state takes care of public health and provides the means of prevention and treatment by building different types of hospitals and medical institutions.

Article 32:

The State cares for the handicapped and those with special needs and ensure their rehabilitation in order to reintegrate them into society. This shall be regulated by law.

Article 34:

First: Education is a fundamental factor in the progress of society and is a right guaranteed by the state. Primary education is mandatory and the state guarantees to eradicate illiteracy.

We had an opportunity to win the hearts and minds of people around the globe, and what we demonstrated instead was that we don't have a vision with which to inspire the rest of the world. This constitution is an example of collectivism, authoritarianism, and legislated subservience—evidence that we are leading the world into democratic socialism. This is how future generations around the globe, are getting the thousand pound gorilla imposed on their backs that leads eventually to injustice, disparity, poverty, and economic collapse.

How could this have happened? Either these politicians never read the US Constitution or they did not want to use legitimate values and ideals as the basis for how people govern themselves. This is just more evidence of our government's secret plan to keep us all subservient.

Historically, most people have resisted any attempt to force such authoritarian ideas on them. For example, in the 1930s, Russian peasants burned their crops, slaughtered their farm animals, and faced starvation rather than support or cooperate with the demands of a communist state. Such acts of defiance illustrate that people view respect for individual rights as a primary moral value.

> I submit that an individual who breaks a law that conscience tells him is unjust and who willingly accepts the penalty of imprisonment in order to arouse the conscience of the community over the injustice, is in reality expressing the highest respect for law.
>
> Dr. Martin Luther King Jr., *Letter from a Birmingham Jail,* 1963

We should dismantle our weapons of mass destruction; there is no foreign enemy that can subdue, defeat, or enslave America. Our greatest threat and enemy is within: *within* our institutions of higher education and *within* each of us, by our failure to stand up and do the right thing. Government is not the problem. The problem is 300 million Americans (most of whom claim to cherish freedom) who support, work with, and depend on the corruption that government now represents. And the truth is, there is no justification for living like doormats.

Education that defines the opportunities, expectations, convictions, and principles that enable everyone to make the most of their life—the key to their future. Websites should be made available for anyone to post educational materials on subjects like character education, reading, writing, arithmetic, and science—information necessary for society to flourish. Such education would be provided around the globe at almost no cost to anyone.

We can build a New World where our technological competence would be matched by our moral values. We can build a nation where people face reality with honesty and confidence, a world where people would act with integrity, purpose, and respect for those around them. People would not live in fear of crime, violence, and corruption. When something afflicted their lives or the lives of those they cared about, responsible adults would find ways to address the problem rather than electing politicians who make hollow promises. Problems like pollution, cultural inequities, population growth, deficit spending, corporate corruption, abortion, discrimination, drug abuse, the health crisis, and mediocre education would be addressed by each citizen as a personal responsibility. The nightly news would report on our successes instead of exacerbating the problems. The future of our nation would be in its people's hands, and they would respond, knowing that nothing is more important than achieving something in life and laying the foundation for a better future for everyone.

I know this is not going to be easy. But if we fail to change course, then five years from now—by 2018—the thousand-pound gorilla on our backs will be a fifteen-hundred-pound gorilla. Just like those Russian peasants who faced starvation rather than cooperate with a communist state, we have to stop being gullible pawns, accepting bailouts, and subsidies, including Social Security benefits. There is no excuse for such complicity with the growing government corruption. We must stop making excuses and refuse to be obedient subjects living on the backs of our neighbors, children, and future generations.

When parents, teachers, intellectuals, and high school students can define the qualities of character required to achieve all that we want in life, the new world will be achieved. The biggest hurdle will be recognizing that it does not require more government—but that each of us discover and nurture moral courage within ourselves.

Young people of America, you must correct my generation's mistakes. You may have cell phones and computers, but you have not been taught the virtues and values that would build a thriving middle class.

Young people, you can lead the way in securing a better future for your children. You can rise above the lies, evasions, and distortions being taught and practiced. You can break the silence and wipe out the pessimism and cynicism that hang over America. You can lead the way out of the confusion and into the light. You can become the leaders of a new world. The dawn of a new kind of civilization, with moral ideals, genuine equality, and justice for all, awaits your leadership. Living in a state of apprehension and doubt, and incessant boredom is not the path you what to follow.

Boredom is the first taste of nothingness. For boredom leads instantly to "killing time." For the bored, no action is more attractive than any other. The self cannot be drawn into action; it lives by and for distraction; it waits. The world acts; the self is acted on. Besides boredom, there is the collapse of a strongly inculcated set of values. I have heard students say with bitterness that high school is "enough betrayal for a lifetime." But after that, what? Social scientists leap in to tell the adolescent that everything is relative, that everything is determined, and to suggest that the social system is the source of his inner emptiness. It is not only the large, impersonal bureaucracy that engenders feelings of helplessness. It is also the recognition that those who wield power are also empty.

Michael Novak, *The Experience of Nothingness,* 1970

Lesson 9: Now it is up to each of us.

What do you think? Should we live in a free society, or do you agree with Harvard professor Michael Sandel, who says, "I do not think freedom of choice—even freedom of choice under fair conditions—is an adequate basis for a just society."

The question is: Are we going to find the courage to do what has to be done, or are we going to rely on more talk with no substance?

One more question: Are you now smarter than your average college professor?

Appendix

For the first 150 years or so of our nation's life, Americans kept reliance on government to a minimum. Then the national foundational economic principles got reversed, and beginning in the 1930s, the cost and size of government began to multiply. The social/welfare policies following the Great Depression became accepted practice. There were occasional deficits—insufficient revenues to pay for government programs—but during World War II the American people were willing to make necessary sacrifices and capable of bearing the cost of their public obligations. After the war, however, reliance on government became accepted public policy.

America recovered from the Great Depression convinced that government programs are what saved them. That was when the self-anointed, want-to-be emperors started to parade around in clothes made of invisible thread, and the nation was duped into believing that these men were leading the nation in the right direction. The nation bought into the presumption that all we need is top-down management to solve our problems. Then along came President Lyndon Johnson (1963-69), who built the Great Society on the backs of taxpayers. His administration brought us Medicare, Medicaid, the War on Poverty, and un-necessary military interventions (the Vietnam War).

Individual expectations and constitutional government were replaced by mandatory servitude. The values, ideals, and principles on which healthy communities must be built were abandoned; instead, Americans obeyed the rulers up on stage.

It was then that the idea of personal character as a guiding vision ceased to exist. No politician or national leader since has dared assert that the solution to our country's problems is a return to reliance on individual initiative and personal responsibility. Since then the nation has grown into a massive bureaucracy funded by growing taxes and serving the military/ financial/corporate/welfare-state complex.

During the Reagan administration (1981-89), free-market ideology (unrestrained behavior, borrowing and spending) became America's religion, and "trickle-down economics" was the new rage. Limited government and unrestrained spending devoid of any moral values were supposed to guide the nation. Free-market ideologists proclaimed that if we just let businesses and consumers (and players in the new global economy) do as they pleased, the economy would prosper. Instead of acting like responsible citizens, we became a nation of consumers, embracing bad habits and fancy excuses.

Americans were given a big tax cut, which helped feed the growing economy; deficit spending became national monetary policy; and Social Security taxes were increased so that government had lots of money to spend. Instead of putting those revenues into the promised trust fund for workers when they retired, politicians spent it. The federal government went on a borrowing and spending spree. Politicians couldn't restrain themselves, and Americans embraced their unrestrained governing. The nation spent money on welfare programs and needless wars, subsidized almost anything, and built a massive bureaucracy. That's when we should have realized that the underlying problem was a dire lack of personal accountability. When President Reagan set out to resolve the growing Social Security insolvency problem, the commission he appointed was headed by Alan Greenspan, an admirer of Ayn Rand who should have known what needed to be done. But instead of putting an end to this massive welfare scam, the blue ribbon committee recommended that Social Security benefits and taxes be expanded. Greenspan, along with the rest of the nation, succumbed to groupthink. It was 1982 when America embraced fancy excuses and servitude—and descended into cultural blindness.

Government programs, regulations, bureaucracies, taxes, and special interests (military, financial, and corporate) grew and multiplied like disease-carrying rodents. This bloated system was even given a disparaging nickname: "voodoo economics." Glaringly absent was any understanding of the moral foundation upon which a healthy economy must be built. Public education became an indoctrination machine in which everyone learned that reliance on government is necessary and essential.

The nation's elite classes, educators, commentators, and economists led America down the path to growing consumption that meant, at least for a time, an economic boom. Politicians like economic booms, but runaway spending, borrowing, and inflation and unrestrained distribution of benefits cannot go on indefinitely. I would describe this period as the "living under the dome" or "money grows on trees" fantasy. It was like being on drugs: it sure felt good while it lasted.

Because of the booming economy, during the Bill Clinton administration (1993-2001) the government ran a surplus for the first time in decades. But the passion for corporate subsidies and welfare spending prevailed. Within a few years, interest on the nation's debt was costing taxpayers almost $1 billion a day. America became a nation in debt, faced with an aging population and a less vibrant economy, especially for the middle class. Or, to put it somewhat differently, working Americans burdened with oppressive taxes (and deliberate devaluation of the currency) were struggling just to make ends meet. It became increasingly evident that politicians couldn't fix the problem without drastically cutting spending and providing competent leadership—something they preferred not to do. Living on borrowed money and relying on the widespread redistribution of people's earnings—institutional servitude—had become a habit in America. Now, as we enter the twenty-first century, the American motto apparently is "Kiss your children's future good-bye."

We have seen the charts plotting future government benefits (promised handouts) versus revenues (taxes). There are predictions that Social Security and Medicare obligations will not be funded by 2042. A few years after the turn of the last century, tax cuts for the rich, a growing economy, and the war in Iraq were pumping money into the stock market, but our underlying economic problems were worsening. Since 2008, we've become well aware that our time and credit are running out. The Bush/Obama bailouts alone will cost every adult and child in America something like $15,000 each. That is on top of the $35,000 of debt already imposed on each of us at the end of 2008. I have a political flyer from the 2008 presidential primary that states, "Two Simple Steps: Save Social Security. Preserve and Strengthen Medicare. Vote for Romney."

In his book *Running on Empty,* Peter G. Peterson reports that the Social Security trustees (the people managing the Social Security and Medicare programs) predict that today's young people will be paying 25 to 40 percent of every paycheck just to fund Social Security and Medicare. Those debts represent the thousand-pound gorilla on our children's backs. Clearly, in the second decade of the twenty-first century, personal responsibility has been replaced with artful excuse-making by professors, commentators, politicians, and voters.

The question facing us all: are we going to continue down the path into financial collapse? The only real alternative is to discover the alternative which has never been realized in human history. We must live as responsible adults who know how to avoid another collapse. Our children and grand children are going to know if we stood up and did the right thing or continued to engage in talk with no substance.

My prediction is that some place, in some community people will talk to one another, work together to forge a new path, to accomplish the re-birth of humanity and civilization, the castle built on the hill, built on a foundation of valid moral principles.

Welcome to the future.

The problem isn't what the government is doing in secret.
The problem is what it is doing right in front of
us, with our consent and with our money

After reading this book you will be smarter than
most college professors because you will know
how to answer two questions they can't:

What kind of people are we?
How do we become the best we could be?

www.TurningTheLightsBackOn.com

About the Author

Who is John H. Zaugg?

John was typical of American youth, except for one thing.

Starting in elementary school John had a strange feeling that something was not quite right. There were persistent unanswered questions. A disconnect between what was said and what was done. At that age one does not know what is wrong or even what questions to ask. The unanswered questions or silence, as he liked to describe it, when something like this: Was society trying to build responsible adults or obedient little robots?

He was repeatedly reassured that the answers would be forthcoming. Things were supposed to get better when he graduated and moved on in life. But answers were never forthcoming, the nagging feelings grew more real.

He graduated from college without answers just like the rest of his friends and classmates. The discontent of his childhood had produced an inquiring mind. He learned to adapt to societies programming and bureaucracy but was repulsed by the regimentation. He was raised by non-disciplinarian parents who never threaten or even yelled. They were also very creative and independent thinkers. The problem was they, like most adults, believed that nothing

119

is for certain. That inherent doubt was the given to be endured. How can a rational being function intelligently if the world is presumed unintelligible or people are presumed inherently incompetent? John discovered the advantage of self-realization as an alternative to self-abdication and blind obedience.

John identified the virtues that are absolutely essential to healthy human behavior and the preservation of human liberty. Because these ideas are not new but deliberately concealed from us, he authored a book unlike any thing in America today. John views himself as playing a role similar to Paul Revere. At stake is nothing less that the ideals on which our success has been built, and on which our children and grandchildren's future depends.